MW01172942

REAL ESTATE REALIST

The No-Nonsense Guide to Rental Property Investing

by
S.J. PLOTKIN

Copyright © 2024 S.J. Plotkin

All rights reserved. No part of this publication may be reproduced, distributed, or transmitted in any form or by any means, including photocopying, recording, or other electronic or mechanical methods, without the prior written permission of the publisher, except in the case of brief quotations embodied in critical reviews and certain other noncommercial uses permitted by copyright law. Any perceived slight against any individual is purely unintentional. Although the author and publisher have made every effort to ensure that the information in this book was correct at press time, the author and publisher do not assume and hereby disclaim any liability to any party for any loss, damage, or disruption caused by errors or omissions, whether such errors or omissions result from negligence, accident, or any other cause. The content of this book is for entertainment purposes only. Neither author nor publisher accepts any responsibility for the results of any actions taken on the basis of information in this book. Author and publisher expressly disclaim all and any liability and responsibility to any person in respect of the consequences of anything done or omitted to be done by such person in reliance, whether wholly or partially, upon this book. For permission requests, write to the publisher at contact@identitypublications.com.

Library of Congress Control Number: 2024903080

ISBN-13: 978-1-945884-83-2 (paperback)

ISBN-13: 978-1-945884-84-9 (hardcover)

First edition, published by Identity Publications.

Editor: Gregory V. Diehl

CONTENTS

INTRODUCTION

Ferris Bueller, in all his infinite wisdom, once told us, *"Life moves pretty fast. If you don't stop and look around once in a while, you could miss it."*

I believe that those who are interested in building wealth should partake in real estate property investing as early as possible. But that doesn't mean you have to be young to get going. It could be any point in your life. The income you derive from owning rental properties helps you start living the life you want and allows you to focus your time on what you want to be doing. Rental property investing can give you freedom and control in your life.

If you already own real estate, great! Some of the information you will glean in this book will show you how to unlock additional rental value and equity in your property via recommendations, technologies, and new laws to maximize your advantage.

PSYCHOLOGICAL FACTORS IN REAL ESTATE INVESTING

Investing in real estate involves a significant amount of psychological factors that can impact your success. Understanding your own mindset, risk tolerance, and emotional intelligence is crucial to making informed decisions and adapting to the ups and downs of the market. Throughout this book, we'll discuss strategies for overcoming common psychological barriers, such as fear of failure, analysis paralysis, and decision fatigue, and help you develop a strong, resilient investor mindset.

Living well is viewed by some as the accumulation of material wealth, often represented by images of Lamborghinis, yachts, designer clothes, mansions, or other physical manifestations of what it means to be rich. Material wealth refers to the possession of physical goods and assets with monetary value, such as money, property, and valuable objects. Some alternate words for material wealth I use in this book include assets, riches, fortune, wealth, possessions, property, and treasure.

However, material wealth is only one aspect of wealth. Other forms of wealth include intellectual wealth (knowledge and education) and spiritual wealth (inner peace and contentment). People's status or social cues are often assumed from these physical representations of wealth. But there's no reason wealth has to look this way if you don't care about displaying it like this.

Those with financial wealth may choose to spend time on personal growth and self-actualization in pursuit of the arts, aesthetics, or sports. Or they may simply wish to give back to the world. With means come options. Those with fewer means must devote more of their time and energy to satisfying deficiency needs, as discussed in Maslow's hierarchy of needs. I believe in you, and you should believe in yourself. All other things being equal, why would you not choose to live a life with more options to pursue what you want? One where you can do things you care about, explore places that most people will never get to see, experience cultures that most people never even know of, and so forth?

Are you ready to become a real estate mogul and create serious wealth for yourself and your loved ones? Investing in real estate can be a fantastic way to achieve financial stability and reach your long-term goals. Whether you want to live comfortably in retirement or use your wealth to make a positive impact on the world, it's important to align your investments with your values and aspirations.

Maybe you're passionate about environmental sustainability. In that case, you might consider investing in green buildings or properties with eco-friendly features. Perhaps you're a history buff who loves the charm and character of older homes. In that case, you might want to focus on buying and renovating historic properties.

I've always seen material wealth as an opportunity to follow our ambitions and accomplish the things we consider most important. Investing in rental properties is demonstrably one of the best ways to acquire this freedom in the shortest amount of time. I choose to use my free time being with my family, playing water polo, and starting new businesses. The path I sought for wealth from an early age wasn't about attaining an ultra-high net worth; it was about having control of my own life and time. It was about not being beholden to a clock, a boss, or anyone or anything else that could tell me what to do with my life.

Forget the arbitrary numbers society sets for what it means to be "wealthy." True wealth isn't about having a certain amount of money. It's about having the financial freedom to live the life you want. That means having a steady stream of cash flow that covers your expenses and allows you to save for the future. Don't get caught up in the hype of huge sums like $1 million or $100 million. In a hundred years, those numbers might not even be considered impressive. Focus on building a strong foundation of cash flow and watch your wealth grow over time.

One of my motivations for writing this book is that I've found a pathway to greater financial freedom and a fuller life. I want to share that path with others who would benefit from it.

Here are a few things to keep in mind if you are working toward owning a rental property:

TIP #1: START SMALL

You don't have to start with a large, expensive property. Consider starting with a smaller property or even a room in your own home that you can rent out. This can help you build up experience and save money for a larger property in the future.

TIP #2: LOOK FOR WAYS TO SAVE MONEY

There are many ways to save money when buying and maintaining a rental property, such as by negotiating a lower purchase price, using energy-efficient appliances, and performing your own maintenance and repairs.

TIP #3: EXPLORE FINANCING OPTIONS

Many financing options are available to help you buy a rental property, even if you don't have a lot of money saved up. Look into options like owner financing, government programs, and crowdfunding platforms.

TIP #4: SEEK OUT SUPPORT

Surround yourself with supportive people who can encourage and help you along the way. This could be friends and family, a mentor, or a local real estate group.

Overall, owning a rental property is a realistic and attainable goal for anyone willing to do the work and make smart financial decisions. Don't let financial barriers hold you back from pursuing your dream of being a landlord.

Nobody knows what tomorrow will bring. If you read this book, hopefully, you'll be able to achieve some of the same success I have (and then some). Hopefully, you'll spare yourself some of my mistakes. You'll understand some of the concepts earlier than you otherwise would have and explore them in your own way. Then, you'll be able to go on to live a life of meaning, purpose, and what matters to you.

No matter your motivations for investing in real estate, it's crucial to do your research and make informed decisions. With careful planning and a bit of luck, you could be well on your way to becoming a successful real estate investor!

CHAPTER 1

KNOW THYSELF, FOR THIS KNOWLEDGE IS POWER

"The only true wisdom is in knowing you know nothing."
—**Socrates**

When I was younger, my dad challenged me to prove my worth and set a goal for myself. He asked me, "Sean, if you're so smart, why don't you have a million dollars?" At the time, I wasn't motivated by greed but by the love and support of a parent. I wanted to show my dad that I was capable of achieving great things. And I did just that, thanks in part to his encouragement.

But even after I reached my goal and proved myself to my dad, I couldn't shake the drive to keep building my own empire. It's not about the money or the end result. It's about the journey and the sense of accomplishment that comes with it. To this day, I still feel the internal fire burning within me to keep pushing myself and striving for success. It's a feeling of can-do-it-iveness that keeps me going, and I wouldn't have it any other way.

Who's supporting you on this path once you decide to get involved in rentals? Have you talked through your vision with the people closest to you, such as your family, friends, and social network? The more you communicate your ambition in a consistent and clear way, the more support you'll get. The more real it will become for you, and the more reinforcement you will receive to make sure your vision becomes a reality. You've got to make it your burning desire and your reality. If you keep it to yourself, you're not out there doing it. You don't feel the pressure and guilt to make it happen. Community support is incredibly important, and many investors overlook it.

By discussing your dreams and visions with those in a position to support you, you help yourself feel confident in your vision. You begin to work through potential obstacles before they arise. Opening up and putting your dream out there causes you to be more accountable for making it real. I love discussing my crazy themes, ideas, and visions with anyone willing to listen with an open mind. By placing my thoughts and goals in the air, others more experienced or knowledgeable than me can calibrate me on a better path to achieve my goals or even recalibrate my goals entirely. Being fixed on one path could be helpful, but it could also prevent you from achieving beyond what you even anticipated at the onset.

No matter how old you are, real estate is something that can grow with you throughout your life, helping to augment passive income, provide tax benefits, improve your credit, act as a hedge against inflation, and give you pride in your ownership. Most importantly, once your wealth goals have been achieved, you will have the freedom to spend your life focusing more intently on whatever matters most to you, whether it be family time, vacations, exploration, or simply being free from the burden of employment. The beauty of rental income is that when it comes and all bills are handled properly, it becomes remarkably reliable unless there are physical disasters or massive regulatory changes.

Income property is an IDEAL investment, which stands for Income, Depreciation, Equity, Appreciation, and Leverage. Not every real estate deal offers these benefits, but the right ones will. Rental property produces income in the form of monthly rent payments and other paid amenities you offer tenants. It offers tax benefits from depreciation on the property (though not the land) as it incurs wear and tear throughout the year. It builds equity as you pay off your mortgage, and you own more and more of the actual property. Rental property also tends to appreciate over time due to inflation and an increasing population that is looking more and more for fewer places to live.

And finally, rental properties give you leverage because the arrangement you make with the bank enables you to acquire it with relatively little of your own money on the line. If you can get banks to lend you money against the property, you can get significantly greater returns on your equity and cash-on-cash returns. If you put $1 into a $100 building and you make a dollar, you've already made your money back with a 100% cash-on-cash return. If you had to put in the full $100 to get the building and made the same $1, it would be only a 1% cash-on-cash return. Keep in mind that that's a loose interpretation and doesn't even consider the enhancement value, returns of future cash flows, tax benefits, etc.

I: Income from rental property is generated through cash flow, or the money remaining after paying for the loan, vacancy, and operating costs. Investors can maximize their income and build wealth through rental properties by selecting properties with high cash flow potential. These investments can be self-sustaining and provide a source of ongoing income.

D: Depreciation allows owners of rental properties to claim a tax deduction for the wear and tear on their property over time. The IRS permits a deduction of 27.5 years for building improvements, reducing adjusted gross income on the tax return. For example, a $275,000 improvement can be deducted at a rate of $10,000 per year. Other expenses and improvements may also be eligible for tax deductions.

E: Equity in a property is the value minus the loan. Holding the property longer can increase equity through loan repayment and appreciation. Property value and equity can be affected by economic changes and are usually determined when the property is sold.

A: Appreciation refers to the increase in the value of a property over time. Rental properties tend to appreciate in value, often outpacing inflation and maintaining their value even during economic downturns. This appreciation can be a valuable hedge against inflation and a source of long-term wealth for investors. Additionally, investing in rental properties allows you to take advantage of market trends and potentially increase the value of your property through renovations and improvements.

L: Leverage in real estate allows investors to control a larger asset with a smaller amount of their own money, potentially increasing their return on investment. However, leverage also increases the risk of a financial loss if the value of the property decreases or the investor can't make loan payments.

The level of freedom that rental property investing offers isn't something you can easily accomplish with most other income sources, no matter how rich they might make you. Even if you have a profession that pays a good salary or hourly wage, such as a doctor or lawyer, most of your time will be eaten up in your pursuit of the wealth it generates for you. You will be beholden to your role for most of your waking life and productive years. That's what prompts many people who have already found success and accumulated wealth in such professions to begin investing in rental properties. They aren't doing it just to add more money to their personal stack; they want to finally develop sources of cash flow that will leave them free to spend their time doing what they really want with it. You can't buy more time, but you can do a lot to regain control of it.

FIRST STEPS

There are several steps to gain experience and knowledge in the field of real estate investing. One option is to work in a related industry, such as property management, real estate, or landscaping. Other jobs that can provide relevant experience include handymen, HVAC technicians, landscapers, housekeeping staff, and building inspectors. These roles involve tasks like home repair and maintenance, HVAC system installation and repair, grounds maintenance, cleaning and upkeep, and building inspection to ensure safety and code compliance. By gaining practical experience in these areas, you can learn the ins and outs of managing and maintaining rental properties.

Another way to gain experience in real estate investing is to find a job within the field itself. This can allow you to earn an income while learning the ropes of the industry. There are many fields within real estate, including construction, sales, lending, and various types of property to specialize in, such as commercial, retail, and industrial. It is important to consider which path will best suit your strengths, interests, and goals, as each comes with risks and rewards. Take the time to carefully research your options to find the best fit for you.

Rental properties attract a diverse range of people. One of the sectors that the most interest comes from is the various trades: plumbers, builders, electricians, painters, and so on. Reliable and skilled tradespeople often make great real estate investors. They have a good understanding of the physical components of properties, such as different building styles, stages of construction, and common building faults and rectification of these. They speak the same language, so they know how to best communicate with other tradespeople to organize and schedule maintenance work. They know the technical terms used in construction and can quickly read and understand building plans. Whether you are managing rental properties or interpreting an off-the-plan development for a sale, this is a valuable skill.

Tradies are also tuned into safety. This knowledge can be invaluable, especially as an owner. A competent tradesperson will strongly grasp what makes for quality client service. They get back to people on time, communicate about projected timelines and costs, and explain the work performed. When a problem does occur, a good tradesperson will use their lateral thinking, experience, and skills to quickly identify the problem, solve the issue, or resolve the situation with strong conflict resolution skills. A successful tradesperson is usually prepared for problems and can identify the source of a problem and develop a way to address it. Problem-solving and risk management skills are key to success in rental investing.

Beyond the trades related to the physical construction and maintenance of properties, plenty of design, legal, and administrative jobs offer relevant experience to future rental property investors. These include accountants, interior designers, real estate attorneys, clerks, secretaries, receptionists, maids, cleaning crews, etc. Think of the auxiliary and supporting roles in any organization, the ones that are not directly in the fight making the big cheese. They are the quiet roles that are just as necessary to the success of the operation. All undergo professional experiences that prepare them in different ways for the realities of managing rental properties successfully. You should start wherever your interest naturally takes you and you see an opportunity to learn while earning a living.

If you've taken the time to become a real estate agent, then one of the best ways you can be prepared to make a deal is by spending time on a multiple listing service (MLS), such as CoStar or LoopNet. An MLS is a database used by real estate brokers to share information about various properties for sale so that they can connect buyers to sellers. Cooperating agents will share commissions on deals made through the MLS.

You could join a real estate association that will allow you to talk with others already involved in this area. Getting started could be as simple as pooling money together with a couple of buddies to renovate an old-income property in a bad area at a great price. Suddenly, though, every time there's a plumbing leak, you need to drive an hour out of your way and deal with tenant complaints, but at least you're getting the experience of dealing with the business. From this experience, you learn how to keep people happy, what the contractors are going to say or how they will bill you, what dealing with a management company is like, or the trials of trying to manage it on your own.

The world of real estate is full of surprises, and even the most experienced investors can't predict everything. But as you gain more experience and an understanding of how the market works, you'll start to see the big picture more clearly. You'll be able to identify opportunities, avoid pitfalls, and be better equipped to handle the unexpected. When things don't go as planned, those little details usually trip us up. So make sure you do your homework, get a thorough inspection, and don't be afraid to negotiate for credits when fixing a property. With a little bit of knowledge and a lot of tenacity, you can turn any deal into a win.

In real estate, the most important thing is to keep playing the game. You never know when a deal that seems like a dud will turn into a home run. That's why it's important to always be learning, negotiating, and adapting. The more you play, the more you'll learn about the ins and outs of the game, and the better you'll become at spotting those hidden opportunities. So don't be afraid to take a chance on a deal that seems too good to be true—it might just be the one that makes all the difference.

It's no secret that we're in a bit of an economic downturn right now (no matter what the Fed or the president might say). But that doesn't mean that real estate deals are completely out of reach! In fact, I've been involved in 15 deals in the past few months that I couldn't close on. Some people might see this as a disappointment, but I see it as a chance to stay sharp and keep my finger on the market's pulse. I know the current valuations and am always ready to strike when the right opportunity presents itself. So don't get discouraged—keep your hunting gear polished and be ready to make that killer deal when it comes your way!

Ready to become a top-notch real estate investor? Great! Your personality or strengths don't matter—you can learn to develop the key traits that every successful investor needs. And one of the most important is detachment. No, I don't mean that you should ignore your gut feelings about a property. But you should also be able to look at the data and make decisions based on universal principles that will help you turn a profit. This discipline applies to all forms of investing, not just real estate. If you're investing in gold, for example, it should be because you understand the financial benefits, not just because you like the way it looks. So don't let your emotions cloud your judgment—learn to make smart, data-driven decisions, and you'll be on your way to real estate success!

When it comes to investing in multifamily properties, the goal is always to make a healthy return on your money. But here's the thing: It can't just be about the money to succeed in real estate. In fact, I believe that having a non-financial sense of purpose should be the driving force behind your actions, not just an afterthought. This higher purpose might be different for everyone—maybe it's about providing comfort and security for your family, or maybe it's about helping others by building something useful. The key is to know yourself and tap into your inner strength. So don't just focus on the financial rewards—find your purpose and let it guide you to success in real estate!

"The road to real estate success is paved with action, not analysis. Don't let paralysis by analysis hold you back from taking that first step. Even if you end up being wrong, the best way to learn and course-correct is by getting started. Trust me; you'll be more knowledgeable than you were before. No one can predict every problem that will come up, not even the experts. But if you refuse to do anything at all because you can't be certain of everything that will happen, you have no chance of fixing those problems and finding success. So don't be afraid to take that first step—it's the key to unlocking your potential in real estate."

Success in real estate investing doesn't depend on your personality type. Whether you're outgoing or introverted, a careful planner, or a risk-taker, there are strategies that can work for you. It's important to identify your strengths and use them to your advantage in the real estate industry. For example, an extrovert may enjoy building relationships with agents and brokers, while an introvert may prefer to work behind the scenes, analyzing market trends and developing strategies. Someone who is highly observant may excel at identifying necessary repairs and renovations, while someone who is abstract and strategic may be able to see untapped potential in a property and find innovative ways to add value. In order to achieve success in the real estate industry, it's important to focus on building skills and abilities in the Executing, Influencing, Relationship Building, and Strategic Thinking domains. These may include tasks such as identifying and evaluating potential properties, negotiating deals, persuading others, building relationships, and thinking critically and strategically about long-term goals and plans. Whatever your personality and strengths, it's possible to find success in real estate investing by being open to learning and adapting to new situations.

BREAK FREE FROM THE PAST

It is very important to consider the mental narrative and barriers that may subconsciously hold us back from pursuing freedom as effectively as we can. This can be the key to overcoming reluctance to get started and gaining real self-confidence. Most of our core beliefs about how accumulating wealth works were put in us in childhood. We probably aren't even aware of what they are or where they came from. We just take them in as a working part of the culture about money that we are exposed to, and they tend to stay with us for life unless we can learn to consciously re-assess them.

Pursuing financial freedom requires overcoming mental barriers and negative beliefs about wealth. These beliefs are often subconsciously adopted in childhood and can hold us back from achieving our goals. To overcome these barriers, it's important to reassess our beliefs and adopt a proactive mindset. A helpful reminder of this can be found in the quote from the movie Once Upon a Time in Mexico, "Are you an Ameri-Can or an Ameri-Can't?"

It's also important to recognize that the accumulation of wealth can enhance personal freedom and the ability to make a positive impact on the world. In some cultures, there may be negative biases surrounding money and the desire for wealth, but it's important to challenge these beliefs and pursue financial success in a way that is meaningful and fulfilling.

Saving money is an important first step toward investing in real estate. It's also important to remember that we don't have to replicate the behavioral patterns of our parents or society, and we have access to different knowledge, talents, and opportunities than they did. We can challenge the belief that wealth and nobility are incompatible and view money as a pathway to spending more time on things we care about and with the people we care about. The wealthiest people often have a long-term goal of becoming wealthy and are willing to work hard and think strategically to achieve it. They also recognize the importance of continuous learning and growing and seek out mentors and advisors who can provide guidance and support. By adopting these habits and beliefs, we can increase our chances of achieving financial freedom.

Crede quod habes et habes—believe that you have it, and you have it. Or, if you prefer it another way: Fake it until you make it. The new reality follows naturally from your confidence that it will be yours. What you believe in becomes your reality. We create our future by how we think, as our thoughts become our actions. That is the power of autosuggestion—our ability to consciously affect our development by feeding our own minds targeted ideas, feelings, and images.

Fear can paralyze us and prevent us from taking the necessary risks to achieve our goals. Self-doubt can cause us to question our abilities and make us hesitant to pursue opportunities that could lead to success. Are you afraid of failure or rejection? Are you afraid of making a mistake that could cost you money? Understanding the root cause of your fears and doubts can help you to develop strategies for managing them.

Adapting to change and uncertainty is essential for success in the real estate industry. Investors who are not able to adapt may miss out on new opportunities or be left behind in a constantly evolving market. To embrace change and uncertainty, it's important to cultivate a mindset of flexibility and openness. This involves being willing to take calculated risks, which means assessing a decision's potential risks and rewards before making it. It also involves being open to new ideas and perspectives, which means being willing to listen to and learn from others. This can include attending industry events, networking with other professionals, or seeking out the advice of a mentor.

Developing a mindset of flexibility and openness takes time and practice. It requires a willingness to step out of one's comfort zone and take risks. However, the rewards can be significant. By being open to change and uncertainty, investors can identify new opportunities and stay ahead of the curve in a constantly evolving market.

Remember that setbacks and failures are inevitable. The ability to handle these challenges in a constructive way is essential for long-term success. Investors who are able to reframe failures as learning opportunities and focus on the lessons that can be gained from them are better positioned to succeed in the long run. One way to do this is by analyzing what went wrong and using that information to improve future decisions. This could involve gathering feedback from clients, analyzing market data, or seeking advice from a mentor or coach. It's also important to focus on the positive aspects of the experience, such as the lessons learned, the new skills acquired, and the growth resulting from the setback.

Resilience is another important aspect of handling setbacks and failures. Resilience is the ability to bounce back from adversity and persevere in the face of challenges. It involves developing a growth mindset and maintaining a positive attitude even in the face of setbacks. One way to develop resilience is by focusing on the things that are within one's control and taking small steps towards progress each day.

Building confidence and assertiveness is crucial for real estate investors who want to succeed in a competitive and fast-paced industry. Confidence enables investors to make sound decisions, negotiate effectively, and take calculated risks. Assertiveness, on the other hand, allows investors to communicate their needs and boundaries effectively, build strong relationships, and lead teams successfully.

Developing a long-term perspective is also crucial for developing patience and perseverance. Real estate investing is not a get-rich-quick scheme, and investors must be willing to commit to their investment strategies over the long term. This means not getting discouraged by short-term setbacks or fluctuations in the market but instead staying focused on their long-term goals. Investing in real estate is a slow process, and investors may not see significant returns for months or even years. Celebrating small successes can help investors stay motivated and feel a sense of accomplishment, which can help them develop patience and perseverance.

Real estate investing is a dynamic industry that is always evolving, and successful investors need to stay current and adapt to new trends, regulations, and market conditions. This requires a continuous learning mindset, where investors always seek out new information, learn new skills, and develop new strategies to help them succeed.

Cultivating a growth mindset is an essential part of continuous learning. A growth mindset involves embracing challenges and seeing them as opportunities to learn and grow rather than obstacles to be avoided. This means taking risks, trying new things, and learning from mistakes and failures.

Attending events and conferences can help investors stay up-to-date with the latest industry trends and gain insights from experts in the field. Industry publications can also provide valuable information on new laws, regulations, and market conditions. Mentors, too, can offer guidance and support and share their own experiences and insights. Coaches can provide valuable feedback and help investors to develop new skills and strategies.

COMMON MISTAKES AND PITFALLS IN REAL ESTATE INVESTING

Real estate investing can be a rewarding and lucrative endeavor, but it's essential to be aware of common mistakes and pitfalls that could jeopardize your success. By understanding these risks and taking steps to avoid them, you can increase your chances of making sound investments and maximizing your returns.

- Failing to conduct thorough research: Before investing in a property, make sure you understand the local market, comparable properties, and potential risks. This will help you make an informed decision and avoid costly mistakes.
- Underestimating costs: Many investors underestimate the costs associated with owning and managing rental properties, such as repairs, maintenance, and vacancies. Be realistic about your expenses and factor them into your calculations when evaluating potential investments.

- Overleveraging: While leverage can be a powerful tool for real estate investors, overleveraging can lead to financial ruin. Make sure you have a solid financial cushion and avoid taking on too much debt.
- Ignoring property management: Property management is a critical aspect of successful real estate investing. Neglecting this responsibility can lead to tenant issues, property damage, and legal problems. Consider hiring a professional property manager or developing a solid plan for managing your properties yourself.
- Emotional decision-making: Avoid making investment decisions based on emotions or personal preferences. Instead, focus on the data and make rational, informed choices that align with your long-term financial goals.
- Lack of diversification: Don't put all your eggs in one basket. Diversify your real estate portfolio to spread risk and increase your chances of success.
- Impatience: Real estate investing requires patience and a long-term perspective. Don't expect to get rich quick or be discouraged by short-term setbacks. Stay focused on your goals and be willing to adapt your strategies as needed.

CHAPTER 2

FAIL TO PREPARE, PREPARE TO FAIL

"Success is walking from failure to failure with
no loss of enthusiasm."
—Winston Churchill

Now that you understand your strengths and your motivation to be successful in rental properties better, it's time to start making a plan rooted in reality for how you're going to get out of the armchair and into some properties. If you fail to prepare, you're ultimately just preparing to fail. My belief is that preparing well comes down to getting your credit together, getting your income sources together, getting your down payment together, and having a basic idea of the market you want to be in.

To build up a down payment for their first real estate investment, a new investor should set SMART goals and create a concrete plan to achieve them. For example, they might set a goal of saving 10% of their income each month for the next year and create a budget and plan for how they will save and invest their money. They should also focus on living within their means, avoiding bad debt, and using credit responsibly. By setting goals, creating a plan, and taking consistent action, an investor can effectively build up the down payment needed to make their first property purchase. Set Specific, Measurable, Achievable, Relevant, and Time-bound goals (SMART goals)

It is impossible to know exactly what the future holds, and those who claim to be able to do so may be attempting to deceive you. The best way to prepare for the future is to carefully study, plan, and take small, incremental actions to shape our destiny. By continuously learning and adjusting our approach, we can improve our understanding of the world and take control of our lives. This approach, which involves constantly adapting and innovating, has helped humanity to progress and improve throughout history. By embracing this mindset, we can avoid becoming bogged down by excessive analysis and instead focus on taking proactive steps toward our goals.

Real estate can be a tool for personal growth and success if approached with a growth mindset. This means being open to learning and adapting rather than having a fixed mindset that resists change. A growth mindset allows us to see failures as opportunities for learning and growth and to build upon our previous experiences to tackle new challenges. By adopting this mindset, we can overcome our fears and embrace the potential for growth and success in the field of real estate.

Setting specific, achievable goals and taking consistent action toward them is important. We can better visualize and work toward their completion by clearly defining what needs to be done to reach our goals. This focus on goal-setting and action-taking can also translate to other areas of our lives, helping us achieve our desired outcomes in various contexts. High-achievers often utilize the practice of autosuggestion, which involves actively focusing on our goals and allowing them to influence our thoughts and actions. This technique can build self-confidence and drive us toward success when employed effectively.

I have dedicated significant time and effort to understanding the details of each property I invest in. I have analyzed various factors, such as property tax records, purchase dates, loan amounts, financing institutions, and refinancing history, to gain insight into the decision-making processes of both agents and sellers. This careful research has helped me make informed and calculated investments. I have also compared recent transactions in the area to gauge the value of a property and determine a fair price for both buying and selling. By studying and staying informed about the market, I have taken advantage of opportunities and made profitable investments, whether through flipping properties or improving and managing them for long-term gain. However, it is important to note that this level of research and analysis may not be suitable for everyone and can potentially lead to paralysis by analysis if not approached with a clear plan and goal in mind.

Fortune favors the prepared mind. With an eye on the prize of digesting the data, I was better suited to recognize and pounce when the right opportunity struck. I was able to know comparable sales from recent transactions in the area to justify a much higher price when I sold it compared to the amount I paid when I bought it. I was able to demonstrate and even argue the spread competently. The majority of buyers don't do that, but the seasoned and skillful ones do. The majority of buyers don't take the actions needed to be prepared and lack the wherewithal, the knowledge, or the ability to do all that. If you want to be uber successful, the time must be put in to become an expert, and this can be best attained by working in the rental property industry in some way.

One of the reasons I could continue from the start of my foray into rental properties is that I spent a couple of hours a day going through every property that came on the multiple listing service. I was well-informed and ready to strike when the proverbial iron was hot. I was young and had a lot of free time to invest in that research. From that, I learned to extrapolate different reasons why properties sold. It was time well spent because that early self-education gave me a strong foundation to be able to take actions that less-informed investors would have considered too risky. I always had a plan to sell for a profit, either soon after buying because I knew I could flip it at a higher price to another buyer looking in the area or after years of improving and managing it. I wouldn't have been able to do these things if I hadn't put in the time.

Now, keep this caveat in mind: You should only undertake this high level of input and research if you aren't the kind of person for whom it won't cause paralysis by analysis and prevent you from getting your foot in the door. I was not paralyzed by my actions because I used the data I obtained to motivate and inform my actions. I could activate and pull the trigger when that opportunity was there because of the preparation I did. When there were no pressing actions to take, no deals to act on, I used that time to study and sharpen my skills. Then I acted when I needed to.

WHAT TO DO IF YOU'RE LACKING FUNDS

My advice to you is to fake it until you make it. Do as much of the work as you can without capital until you are in a position to get it so you will be prepared to act when the opportunity arises. Put in the work to know the properties, the values, and the variation between the top of the market and the bottom. What is the physical distance between areas where properties are selling at $600 per square foot versus areas where they are selling for $300 per square foot?

There's plenty of research and information-gathering work you can do well before you ever put your first down payment on a property. Spend your time finding investors. Scour your local neighborhood rentals so that you can understand the inventory and competition you will be dealing with. Try to understand the subjective appeal of what's available and why some properties are valued so much higher or lower than others. Most importantly, be asking yourself this whole time where you want to be and why you want to be there. When the right deal comes, you'll be ready to act.

Usually, when you start talking about doing something big, new, and potentially risky, you end up getting a lot of pushback from the people in your life. Well, a lot of that tends to die down when those same people who initially resist the idea of change see you out there taking meaningful actions toward your goal. They slowly start to believe in the reality and the logic of what you're doing. And this can be especially important if you ever plan on relying on any of the people in your life, such as friends and family, to co-invest with you on a property.

In order to prepare, you have to be actively trying to transmute your hopes into your reality. This could be finding a job that pays you to be living in the world of real estate and getting exposed to its nuances. If you're a gardener, you're walking the property, seeing what's needed, and talking with the people who live and work there. I have a plumber who has been working at one of my buildings for many years. He's very good at his job. Whenever he's there working, we end up talking shop together. I give him insight into rental property investing, and he gives me tips about his trade, so we both learn something valuable.

That plumber now owns a four-unit apartment building. He asked me recently what the best way to monetize the free laundry room he was providing his tenants would be. I gave him some advice he didn't expect: Ditch the laundry room entirely and convert the space into an accessory dwelling unit that you can rent out to more tenants. Then, put laundry appliances in each unit and increase the rent to account for the upgrade. Most tenants prefer having laundry available in their units anyway and will gladly pay an extra $200 per month. That, combined with the extra $1,500 from the new ADU that he converted out of the old laundry room, meant he now had an additional $2,300 monthly cash flow.

PREPARE MORE FUNDS THAN YOU THINK YOU WILL NEED

Plan well in advance to have sufficient funds in the bank to handle planned unit upgrades. If you don't save, you won't be able to remodel your units. Then you'll be dead in the water because most tenants in most areas want good, clean units with modern aesthetics and amenities to live in. If you have to leave your units in bad condition due to a lack of funds for remodeling and renovating, you're left having to compete with other rentals on price. The chances go up that you won't be able to rent the unit at all if it's not in livable condition, which means your vacancies may slowly eat you up, and you'll be further in the hole each day that you're not bringing in much income from rent.

It becomes exponentially harder to operate at a profit in the beginning with a high vacancy rate. If you have one unit and it's vacant, you have 0% occupancy and 100% vacancy. If you have two units and one unit is vacant, you have 50% occupancy. As you ramp up your ownership of units, the vacancy factor goes down.

At the moment, I have a lot of units vacant across my properties, but that's because they are all being remodeled to increase the income greatly from what they produced previously. Once they are ready, I'm going to rent them for substantially more than they were rented for before. I can handle all these vacancies for the time being because I have hundreds of units overall.

My vacancy factor from those remodels is only 2% vacancy. I'm actually still underperforming the expected metric of vacancy, which is 3%–5%.

The 3-5% vacancy rate is typically a good gauge for empirically testing if you are renting your units at the going market rate. Any lower than that might mean that you are not extracting the highest potential rental rate. The rate is calculated by taking the number of vacant units, multiplying that number by 100, and dividing that result by the total number of units. The vacancy rate and occupancy rate should add up to 100%. So, if an apartment portfolio has 1,000 units and 30 units are unoccupied, it means the vacancy rate is 3%.

As well, you can look at general vacancy rates in an area as an indicator of whether rates will go up in the area and whether there's enough demand to justify investing there. The lower the vacancy rate, the better indicator it is for the prospective buyer. Many times, I've bought properties from sellers that proudly boasted they had no vacancies in their units. In these cases, I could deduce with a fair degree of accuracy that I was getting a deal with room for me to raise the rents higher than currently charged. If area vacancy rates are excessively high (such as over 10%), it might indicate general low demand in that area due to a lack of local amenities or that rental rates are too high, or the condition of properties is quite poor.

Bear in mind that renovations can end up taking many months longer than most new property owners anticipate. Most property owners can only handle renovating about one-third to one-half of their units per year, and larger properties with hundreds of units can take a few years to update all their units. It may be prudent to time the renovation of each unit according to when there is a natural uptick in vacancy for any given unit. After all, increased vacancy may be a sign that residents are not willing to rent something in less-than-modern condition.

Beyond basic renovations, it's prudent to have enough money available to repair damages as soon as they are likely to occur. The problem is that there are so many ways a unit can be damaged (either due to tenant behavior or some other cause) that you can't possibly predict, prevent, or prepare for them all. You can suddenly find that your wood floors are falling apart from within due to an unknown termite problem. A tenant can leave a faucet running with a clogged drain and cause water damage. Water heaters can break.

Vandals can break into basements and turn furnaces on full blast in the middle of the night for no discernible reason.

Separately meter your units so that your tenants are incentivized not to waste utilities or be careless with them. A tenant who has to pay for their own utilities will use them one-third less on average. So you're not only saving money, but you're doing good for the environment by conserving resources. And at least you'll know who is causing problems when they do occur. If that's too expensive, pay for segmenting services (which are usually just a nominal fee) that will take your bill and split it amongst your tenants for separate billing. As much multifamily housing is stock master-metered for water and sewer (meaning that the entire building is measured on a single meter), the offer of grants for water efficiency upgrades can be particularly valuable. The act also expands funding for the benchmarking of energy and water use in affordable housing, which will produce a valuable database for road-mapping future efficiency upgrades.

How do you plan how much money to set aside for maintenance, repairs, and other expenses that can occur in each unit you own? It depends on several factors, such as the age of the unit. Newer properties obviously tend to have fewer upkeep costs. As they get older, they are more likely to need something fixed or changed. As well, previous owners may have left you in a position of deferred maintenance on issues that should have already been paid for but now are your burden to resolve. If, however, an older property has recently undergone a major renovation, you can reasonably anticipate not needing to address the aspects that were renovated for some time, such as replaced plumbing and wiring.

Still, there can be costs you won't know to anticipate. I own a building constructed in 1989 that causes me more trouble with roof and gas leaks than many 1920s properties I've owned. Newer buildings aren't always as well built as they once were, and blanket assumptions based on the age of a building don't necessarily hold true.

You'll also have to consider the environment and climate conditions your property is in. Areas with lots of snow will have different upkeep expenses than areas near the beach with salty air.

It's in your best interest to tour every property you are considering buying with a qualified general contractor. They can clue you in not just about the present condition of the building but also about the expected long-term issues you'll need to address (including how much they will cost you on a recurring basis). Hire an independent third party for a property condition assessment report. Do your due diligence now to avoid the nasty surprise of financial commitments you didn't factor into your business model down the road.

There is a big cost difference between a general contractor and a skilled tradesman. The general contractor can give you an accurate understanding of the costs, including insurance and worker's compensation. They help you make more informed decisions as to the shelf life of a property. On a walk-through inspection, there are many perspectives on the effective life of different elements of the property, including but not limited to electrical, plumbing, heating, paint, bathrooms, kitchens, roofs, windows, balconies, stair rails, and water heaters. A competent inspector and/or general contractor can be your eyes and ears to argue most competently and establish a sound paper trail for why your offer should have adjustments to the final price. In the end, it is your and the other party's discretion to take their recommendations and agree to a concession or not.

STUDY YOUR NEIGHBORHOODS

In order to fully understand the value of a rental property, it is important to consider the various sub-neighborhoods within the city. Let's take my favorite city to invest in and list a small selection of the sub-neighborhoods, each with its own distinct character and features. They can vary widely in terms of real estate values and demand. These neighborhoods include but are not limited to Belmont Heights, Alamitos Heights, Wrigley, Rose Park, Belmont Shore, Lakewood Village, Naples, Bluff Heights, East Village Arts District, Westside, Bixby Knolls, Los Altos, Cal Heights, Zaferia, Rancho Estates, and Stearns Park. By thoroughly researching the real estate trends within these sub-neighborhoods, you can better understand the value of a property within a specific area. Additionally, it can be helpful to compare properties that span multiple sub-neighborhoods in order to identify any potential discrepancies in value. By carefully analyzing comparable sales within these areas, you may be able to argue that a property is worth more than its initial asking price based on the value of similar properties in the surrounding area. This type of in-depth research and analysis is crucial for making informed and calculated investment decisions in the Long Beach rental market.

Knowing your neighborhood well can be extremely beneficial for real estate investing. Here are a few reasons why:

Market knowledge: Understanding the local real estate market can help you make informed decisions about which properties to invest in. You'll be able to identify trends and predict how well a particular property is likely to perform in the future.

Networking opportunities: Building relationships with other real estate professionals in your neighborhood can be extremely helpful. You'll be able to learn from their experiences, get insights into the local market, and potentially even find properties to invest in through their networks.

Community involvement: Being active in your community can help you gain a better understanding of the area and its residents. This can be helpful when it comes to finding properties that will appeal to potential renters or buyers.

Property management: If you own rental properties in your neighborhood, being familiar with the area will make it easier for you to manage them. You'll have a better understanding of the types of people who live there and be able to anticipate any potential issues that may arise.

KEEP YOUR CREDIT CLEAN

You can easily get started in real estate at any age, even if you're under 18. You can have a parent, older sibling, or someone who trusts you add you as an authorized user on their credit cards. By doing this, you can build up a $10,000-to-$50,000 credit card limit. This is important because one of the metrics that's used to determine your creditworthiness is your available credit. If you have a $50,000 credit card limit with 100% available credit, the credit reporting agency algorithms (such as those used by Transunion, Equifax, or Experian) deem you more creditworthy. Creditworthiness is an important hoop to jump through if you're looking to get a conventional loan or even if you're looking to get seller financing with the seller lending you their money.

A good real estate agent will always tell you that you need to have a buyer if you're going to be lending them money to have sound credit. You want to have sound credit so that you'll be able to demonstrate that you have made sound financial decisions in the past. Your credit is the most important thing to establish and grow in real estate. In the United States, if you don't have credit, you're not even on the grid. Your investment options are extremely limited, including real estate. To grow your net worth quickly without having to put in your time, you need the option of putting it into real estate. It is the easiest path to financial freedom.

If faced with bad credit, it's usually harder to buy a building. But with preparation, you can benefit from seller financing, which is where the lender is the seller. The seller could be willing to lend to you if they like and/or trust that you won't place their loan in jeopardy. So you don't necessarily need to have great credit, but it helps with coming up with a source for your down payment.

Credit-wise, I was prepared when the opportunity came up for my first purchase. In fact, I got double lucky. My father instilled in me the importance of having great credit even from a young age and helped me to establish credit even as a child. I used this credit to sign and cash a credit convenience check for a decent amount to help with the down payment and a large portion of the repair expenses. As a 20-something still in college, I didn't have the skills to renovate the property myself or the liquid money accessible to pay professionals. So, I devised a plan to barter with tradesmen by trading their work in exchange for free rent in the building. The remaining vacancies were rented slightly under-market (to compensate for the poor state of the units). With bootstrapping principles, no direct experience, little cash, and stellar credit, I was able to hit the ground running.

However, all hope is not lost if you have bad credit. Besides building good credit or fixing bad credit, utilizing a credit reporting agency like Credit Karma, which offers free monitoring, can be helpful. However, for a more comprehensive and robust approach to credit and identity protection, I prefer using Identity Guard through Costco for just $7.99 a month. This paid service offers distinct advantages: Comprehensive Monitoring: Identity Guard monitors your credit reports from multiple bureaus, providing a broader view of your credit activity compared to free services. Advanced Fraud Detection: With advanced algorithms and technology, Identity Guard detects potential signs of fraud quickly and delivers faster alerts compared to free services. Identity Theft Protection: Identity Guard goes beyond credit monitoring, offering features like dark web monitoring and digital security tools for enhanced protection. Dedicated Customer Support: Identity Guard provides access to dedicated support teams that can assist you in resolving identity theft or fraud-related issues. Insurance Coverage: Some Identity Guard plans include identity theft insurance, offering financial protection against eligible losses. Considering these additional benefits, paid credit monitoring services like Identity Guard offer a proactive and comprehensive approach to protecting your credit and identity. While free services can be helpful, investing in a paid service provides greater peace of mind, support, and coverage for your financial well-being.

You typically want to have a 680 credit rating at minimum to be considered a tier-two credit. Ideally, your credit rating would be 720 or above to be tier one. Tier one credit gets the best interest rates, the best deals, the best credit cards, and the best credit lines. It is deemed the lowest risk by lenders and credit card companies, finance companies, and installment loan companies.

For your best chances of success in rental investing, it makes sense to get your credit as strong as possible. However, it is not fully necessary if the right deal presents itself and you can't wait. For FHA, the bare minimum score to qualify is 580 for 3.5% down. Even then, if below 580, you can still purchase with 10% down.

Alternatively, with some form of seller financing in which you convince the seller to help with a small part of the down payment, you can buy a property. With VA (Veterans Administration) financing, there is no minimum credit score, but you are required to live in one of the units. With conventional residential financing, loans are broken into prime, subprime, and three levels between the two. With multi-family financing, the loan's income is the primary concern, but having better credit will get you better rates.

A credit line is a revolving item that can grow as you pay it off. Some steps that I've done in the past to help boost my credit are to apply for additional credit cards to increase the amount available. If I need to use credit, I don't go above 30% utilization. Credit utilization is a main factor in calculating your credit score, and if you have more than 30% of your credit being used, then you will have a large ding on your credit rating, and you will not qualify for the best rate. Then, you won't be able to extract the best loan and get the greatest leverage, which means you won't be able to get the most property that produces the most income and grows your net worth.

INVEST WITH COLLABORATIVE PARTNERS

If you are the sole owner of a property, you have complete control over all decisions related to the investment. However, if you are buying the property with one or more other people, you must consider a variety of additional factors. While having additional people involved in the investment can bring benefits such as added skills and shared risk and responsibilities, it also introduces new challenges and potential liabilities.

It's important for both parties in a property partnership to understand the time commitment involved. Unless the other person's role is solely to provide financial support and not be involved in any other capacity, it's likely that the partnership will require a significant amount of additional time from both parties. This is one of the main reasons why property management companies are successful—many people don't want to add the time requirement and responsibility of managing a property on top of their existing obligations. Everyone's time is valuable, and most people want to focus on their own lives rather than taking on additional responsibilities.

Many newcomers to the field don't understand the time-intensive nature of it. It can easily lead to resentment between partners if one of them feels like they are taking on a larger share of the time burden than the other. One person ends up in the position of having to make most of the critical decisions, having to figure out where to get money from, and having to figure out the best ways to spend that money. Meanwhile, the other partner is mostly ignorant of these processes and why certain strategic choices are being made. They don't know why their partner just spent so much money on repairs and renovations to something they weren't there to witness. Resentment slowly builds, and trust falls apart.

All these grievances can be avoided by clarifying communication and expectations before getting into a real estate partnership with anyone. At the very least, contracts should have clear, measurable criteria. Key milestones and their planned dates should be included. Budget concerns and contingency plans for exceeding them should be outlined. How long do you all agree to hold the property? How will appreciation affect this timeframe? Who's planning to qualify for the loan? This saves a lot of wasted time and frustration, as you won't be arguing back and forth with your partner about what is going on and whether it's what you both agreed to.

Better still, passive resentment won't build between you. Remember that even if you walk away from the deal having made a nice profit, you'd ideally also still like to have the friends you went into it with. In fact, you'd like to be able to continue working with the same people on new opportunities as they emerge. If the relationship works out for everyone, why shouldn't you have the same people primed and ready to engage whenever a promising new deal that suits your respective strengths pops up?

CREATIVE FINANCING STRATEGIES

Creative financing strategies can be a powerful tool for real estate investors looking to build wealth through rental properties. Rather than relying solely on traditional financing methods, investors can use creative financing to secure funding from alternative sources. One strategy is seller financing, where the seller acts as the lender and provides financing for the purchase of the property. Another option is lease-to-own agreements, where the tenant pays rent with an option to buy the property at a predetermined price. Additionally, investors can consider using a private lender or take advantage of government programs such as the FHA 203(k) loan program or VA loan program. These strategies can help investors secure funding that may not be available through traditional lending channels and can be especially helpful for those with limited resources or credit history. However, it is important to carefully consider the terms and risks associated with each financing option to ensure that it aligns with the investor's goals and financial situation.

CHAPTER 3
ALL TYPES AND SIZES

"Size is not a limitation, but rather a challenge to be overcome."
—Arnold Schwarzenegger

Brick-and-mortar real estate is any building you can physically touch. Regardless of what it's actually made of, it is commonly known as "brick-and-mortar" because it is an easy and affordable method for quickly constructing buildings that do not require excessive education or experience. The term refers to the physical aspect that is inherent to real estate.

One of the beautiful things about owning a physical asset like brick-and-mortar real estate is that the land will always have intrinsic value. Land is something that no one is making any more of any time soon, and as the population increases over time, it will become more scarce. Suppose that a property is in a desirable location near an ocean or body of water. In that case, the land itself can commonly be worth more than the "brick-and-mortar" aspect of the building added to the land, which is usually called the improvement to the land.

There are enormous potential benefits to your wealth and freedom that can come from being a prudent rental property owner. But this path has many risks, liabilities, and downsides, even for those who do everything right. There is risk implicit with any type of physical real estate that you don't have with more liquid assets like stocks or bonds. There could be a massive earthquake, or the building could burn down. Someone could slip, fall, injure themselves, and sue you.

Investors in rental properties also need to account for factors like how construction and refurbishment affect the amount of time the apartments may sit vacant and not generate income. When a bank gives a loan, the investor agrees to make payments whether the property generates an income or not. Not to mention, there is a whole range of human behavior risks that a rental property owner exposes themselves to by forming relationships with tenants, who could unintentionally harm themselves, your investment, or your reputation at any time.

Still, rental properties tend to carry fewer risks than other types of real estate you could invest in. They are less affected by changes in consumer demand than office and retail spaces or hotels, for example. With rental property, customers are rebuying the right to your product every month until they move out, and then you get another customer who does the same. It is in your best interest to study and understand the many shapes, forms, and sizes that rental properties come in before just diving headfirst into a large apartment building purchase. Some particular risks and benefits come with each of them. Your best options will depend heavily on the area you are buying in and your personal tastes as an investor.

TYPES OF RENTAL UNITS

An efficiency apartment is a compact and practical rental option that's perfect for solo dwellers. These cozy abodes often feature a multi-functional layout, where the bedroom, living room, and bathroom seamlessly integrate into one open space. Though small in size, efficiency apartments offer great value for money, as the cost per square foot is usually higher than larger units. While some may not come with a full kitchen, these apartments offer a convenient and budget-friendly option for those looking to live alone. If you're looking for a bit more space, a studio apartment could be the perfect fit. These units offer a slightly larger floor plan than efficiency apartments and typically come with a compact kitchen, so you can whip up your favorite meals at home. Studio apartments are a great choice for those who enjoy an open-concept living space and want to keep things simple.

While these smaller units may not have the same appeal as larger, more spacious apartments, they can be the perfect choice for renters who are on a budget or looking for a more low-maintenance living space. For those who want a bit more room to move around, two-bedroom apartments are often the most popular with tenants and cost-effective for landlords to manage. With two bedrooms, these units are ideal for families, roommates, or anyone who wants a bit more privacy and space. With a variety of unit types available, there's something for everyone, whether you're looking for a cozy efficiency apartment or a spacious two-bedroom unit. So, it all depends on your lifestyle and budget!

SINGLE-FAMILY UNITS WITH SEPARATE APARTMENTS

Single-family units can be a useful initial or middle option between owning a home or having to jump to a 5+ multi-family apartment building with greater down payment requirements and higher barriers to entry. Commonly, it's misconstrued that a four-unit apartment building needs all units to be attached to each other and cannot be freestanding spaces of their own. Several properties provide the benefits of feeling separate, perhaps even in up to four separate smaller homes, each with a yard and plenty of space. This might be an option for owners who want to have the benefits of living in a single-family residence but also want apartment rental income. People are sometimes fearful of living in a home and having neighboring tenants. However, as an owner/operator, you can hand-select the tenants to be optimal next-door neighbors with similar lifestyle habits, patterns, and sleeping schedules to your own, thus minimizing the potential for disruption or dispute between you.

DUPLEXES, TRIPLEXES, AND FOURPLEXES

Duplexes, triplexes, and fourplexes (also called quadruplexes) are multi-unit buildings that are becoming increasingly popular as an investment opportunity for those looking to enter the real estate market. They can provide a great opportunity for short-term growth and long-term income streams and be a great alternative for those who may not have the funds available to secure a residential loan. A duplex is a building that contains two separate units, with each unit having its own entrance and living space. A triplex is similar but contains three units, and a fourplex contains four units. These types of multi-unit buildings can be a great option for investors looking to purchase a property and rent out the individual units. The rental income from the units can help cover the mortgage payments and provide a steady income for the property owner.

Additionally, suppose a duplex or triplex is on a similar size parcel as larger units or zoned in a certain way. In that case, you can use the regulations of SB9 to get control of the land itself and split the lot or add one or two accessory dwelling units to the duplex/triplex, thereby maximizing the residential financing at a building cost lower than the cost of purchasing. Overall, duplexes, triplexes, and fourplexes can be great investment opportunities for those looking to enter the real estate market. They can provide a steady income stream, and with the right strategy, they can also provide excellent growth potential.

GARDEN-STYLE APARTMENTS

Garden-style apartments are a popular type of multi-family rental property characterized by their outdoor complexes, greenery, and peaceful suburban location. These properties typically feature between one and three stories of housing, ranging from 50 to 500 units. They are often constructed using wood frame materials and are located in suburban areas where residents can enjoy a quiet and serene environment.

One of the key benefits of garden-style apartments is the convenient access to the building and its amenities. These properties are designed with outdoor spaces in mind, which makes it easy to incorporate amenities such as parking and common areas into the layout. Additionally, tenants appreciate the privacy and distance that garden-style apartments offer, compared to mid-rise and high-rise options where only walls or floors separate residents.

Garden-style apartments also offer residents an abundance of nature and serenity. They typically feature gardens, lawns, and other greenery, as well as beautiful landscapes and interior courtyards. With proper building management and maintenance, these properties can retain their natural look and provide a peaceful environment for residents.

Another advantage of garden-style apartments is the ample space they often offer. This allows tenants to comfortably enjoy both essential and recreational amenities in the building, such as pools or clubhouses. Additionally, many garden-style apartments have private entrances, which plays into the sense of privacy that many people desire in their housing.

The cost of a garden-style apartment can vary depending on factors such as the unit size, location, maintenance routine, and amenities in the building. However, these properties are often located on the outskirts of cities and are, therefore, more affordable than similar options in urban areas. Overall, garden-style apartments offer a unique blend of serenity, natural beauty, convenience, and privacy, making them an attractive option for rental property investors.

MID-RISE APARTMENTS

Mid-rise rental properties, typically located in densely populated urban areas, are a popular investment opportunity for landlords and developers. With between five and nine stories, these buildings are constructed using steel frame technology and are designed to maximize land usage in areas where land is scarce. In these types of buildings, developers have to be more conscious of the height and land area constraints, resulting in smaller units and the need for more efficient land use. Commonly most mid-rise buildings are between 50 and 200 units and employ one of two types of construction options: wrap and podium construction. In wrap construction, the parking area is located in the center of the building, while in podium construction, the parking area is typically located beneath the apartments. Amenities such as gyms, leasing, and commercial centers are often located in the same area, directly below the building.

HIGH-RISE APARTMENTS

High-rise buildings are tall structures that typically have more than ten stories and are constructed using a steel frame. They can be found in urban centers like New York, San Francisco, Los Angeles, and other major cities world-wide. The reason for building high-rise properties is to meet the demand for additional space in densely populated areas with limited land availability. As a result, a high-rise building may have between 150 and 500 units. Due to their location and height, these buildings often come with a high price tag but may not have the same family-oriented amenities found in garden-style properties. Instead, they often include amenities such as fitness centers, business centers, and restaurants, catering to the needs of city dwellers who are accustomed to urban life.

PROPERTY CLASS STRUCTURE

Rental properties are often classified into four different categories: Class A, Class B, Class C, and Class D. These classifications are used to provide investors with an idea of the quality of the property and the type of returns they can expect. Class A properties are newly constructed, have high-end amenities and are located in desirable areas with low maintenance needs. They are often rented to white-collar workers and tend to be more stable investments. Class B properties are older, around 5–15 years old, and have been renovated. They offer a balance between affordability and comfort and target middle-class tenants. Class C properties are usually over 40 years old, contain mostly blue-collar workers and subsidized housing, and have not been renovated in a long time. They offer basic amenities and are often rented to tenants with low disposable income. Class D properties are the lowest quality, located in areas with high vacancy rates, and require intensive management to rent. They may have low upfront costs but can also be challenging to manage.

SPECIALTY MULTIFAMILY TYPES

Specialty Housing refers to multi-family properties that serve specific groups of people, such as students, seniors, or those trying to abstain from drugs, alcohol, or other intoxicants.

Student Housing is accommodation for university students located within a university community, usually rented by a room or bed, and typically short-term leases of 9–10 months. These properties are often subject to damage, so property owners need to set aside more money for repairs and renovations. As student housing becomes more popular, property owners are focusing on student-oriented amenities to increase occupancy.

Senior Housing is becoming more popular due to the aging of the baby boomer generation. It allows for independent living and creates a community for people of the same age. There are three types of senior housing: independent living, assisted living, and nursing home/skilled nursing facilities. Independent living focuses on community interaction and is typically open to anyone over 55. Assisted living is more focused on healthcare and the constant presence of care and medical staff. Nursing homes/skilled nursing facilities cater to seniors who need assistance with nearly all day-to-day activities, 24/7 medical and care services, and rehabilitation.

Sober Living Housing provides accommodation for people trying to abstain from drugs, alcohol, or other intoxicants. These properties feature programs and activities to help occupants beat addiction and maintain abstinence. Some sober living properties allow for the cohabitation of genders, while others only allow for one gender. This type of housing may also have strict rules for occupants' conduct, such as mandatory drug testing or curfews.

Affordable Housing is a type of housing that is available at below-market rates to individuals and families with low or moderate incomes. The goal of affordable housing is to provide safe, decent, and inexpensive residences to people who might not otherwise be able to afford them. Affordable housing can take many forms, such as public housing, vouchers, or tax credits. Affordable housing can also be built by private developers and organizations with funding from government programs or grants. Many affordable housing developments have a mix of units for different income levels, with the majority of units reserved for those with lower incomes.

Workforce Housing is a type of affordable housing intended for people who work in a particular area but may not be able to afford to live there. These properties are targeted toward teachers, firefighters, police officers, and other essential workers who may not be able to afford market-rate housing in the area where they work. Workforce housing can be provided through a variety of programs, such as government-funded affordable housing developments or private developments with financing from state or local government.

Co-Living is a type of shared housing where several individuals live together in a single unit or building. Co-living spaces can be found in single-family homes, apartments, or dormitories, with shared spaces such as bathrooms, kitchens, and common areas. Unlike traditional roommate situations, a property management company often manages co-living spaces and offers additional amenities such as a cleaning service, shared workspaces, and social activities to encourage community building.

GREEN AND SUSTAINABLE PROPERTY INVESTMENTS

As more and more people become aware of the impact of climate change on our planet, the demand for sustainable and green property investments is on the rise. As a rental real estate investor, incorporating sustainable and eco-friendly practices in your properties not only benefits the environment but can also be financially rewarding.

One way to make your rental properties more sustainable is to install energy-efficient appliances and fixtures. These include LED light bulbs, low-flow showerheads and toilets, and Energy Star-certified refrigerators, dishwashers, and washing machines. Energy-efficient appliances not only reduce energy usage but can also lower utility bills for your tenants, making your property more attractive and competitive in the rental market.

Another way to make your rental properties more eco-friendly is to incorporate sustainable materials in your renovation or building projects. This can include using sustainable wood products, such as bamboo or reclaimed wood, or installing solar panels to generate renewable energy for your property. These sustainable practices not only reduce your carbon footprint but can also increase the overall value of your property.

In addition to energy-efficient appliances and sustainable building materials, incorporating green spaces and gardens into your rental properties can also be beneficial. Green roofs and walls, community gardens, and outdoor seating areas not only promote healthy living but can also provide a peaceful and relaxing environment for your tenants.

Finally, offering incentives for environmentally friendly behavior can be a great way to encourage your tenants to make sustainable choices. These incentives can include rewards for reducing energy usage, composting, or even offering free bicycles or public transit passes to reduce carbon emissions.

Incorporating sustainable and green practices in your rental real estate investments not only benefits the environment but can also attract tenants who value sustainable living. By implementing these strategies, you can make a positive impact on the environment while also improving the financial performance of your rental properties.

CHAPTER 4

THE POWER OF LOCATION: YOUR SECRET WEAPON

"The best way to predict the future is to create it."
—Abraham Lincoln

When it comes to investing in rental properties, location can be the ultimate determining factor in the success of the investment. As the saying goes, "real estate is all about location, location, location." The location greatly impacts desirability, rental income, and potential for appreciation.

When choosing a location for your rental property, it's essential to consider the area's demographics. Properties located in areas with a strong rental market, such as areas with a high population of young professionals, students, or retirees, tend to be in high demand. This is because these demographics tend to have a high need for rental properties. Furthermore, properties in areas with a strong job market are more likely to attract long-term tenants and generate higher rental income. This is because these areas tend to have diverse industries, providing job opportunities for a wide range of people and making them attractive locations for renters.

Another important factor to consider when choosing a location for your rental property is the proximity of the property to amenities such as parks, shopping centers, and public transportation. Properties located near these amenities tend to be in high demand as they offer convenience for renters. Additionally, properties located near good schools tend to be in high demand from families, providing a steady stream of renters.

It's also important to research the local rental market to get an idea of the average rent prices in the area. Look for properties that can generate rental income that is above the average market rental price. This will help you to generate a positive cash flow. In addition, look for areas with low vacancy rates, as this indicates a strong rental market and less competition for renters.

Furthermore, research the property taxes in the area and factor them into your budget. High property taxes can eat into your rental income and reduce your potential return on investment. As you can see, there are many factors to consider when choosing a location for your rental property. Considering all these factors, you can increase your chances of finding a profitable rental property that provides long-term financial benefits.

If you're serious about finding a good deal, two tried and true methods of finding off-market deals are sending out postcards and knocking on doors for rentals to tell owners you are interested in their property. "Have you thought about selling? Would you be interested in selling to me? Do you have a price in mind? What would that price be? Well, I've done some research, and I have the comparables, and I would prefer to pay you this."

I love buying real estate in my area of Long Beach because if I want to argue something price-per-unit, what does that really mean? That means I take the sales price or the intended purchase price and divide it by the number of units. But not every deal is apples-for-apples. Some buildings might have 12 studios, which are 12 units. Some buildings might have 12 one-bedrooms, which are also 12 units. Some buildings might have 12 two or three-bedrooms, which are 12 units. You can't always compare buildings in the same area just based on their number of rooms because there could be many other relevant factors to consider in the valuation. For example, maybe one 12-unit studio property was built in 1990, and another was built in 1920.

Each seller is in a different financial position. Typical reasons for closure in real estate are death, divorce, or destitution. Maybe the courts require it. Maybe someone had some bad luck and suddenly went broke. Whatever the reason, they simply need to sell. Different factors at any point in the real estate cycle can cause any property to be sold.

The best bet is usually going directly to the seller to build rapport and a personal relationship. Sit down and take the time to get to know this person. Figure out what it is that motivates them because they may be willing to sell you the property for way less than you would be willing to pay. They may be able to offer you terms to lend you the money to buy their own place because they want to have cash flow.

Deciding where to buy property comes down to a few personal factors for me beyond those mentioned above, the most important of which is where you happen to be based and are comfortable traveling. In countless different ways, it will be important for you to visit your properties habitually and see with your own eyes what is actually going on there (yes, even if you have the best property manager in the world). You definitely don't want to buy something far out of state, something you might not ever visit once the purchase is complete, and hope to set it on autopilot and expect it to work out hassle-free. This is not a "set it and forget it" investment vehicle under even the best of conditions. Most people really don't want to have to drive more than 30 minutes away from where they live. It makes sense to start where you're at and then look for the areas with the best development potential indicators, such as great new restaurants.

When investing in property, think of it as a tightrope act: you're balancing between proximity and profit. It's best to keep your acquisitions within a comfortable driving radius unless you fancy midnight road trips to deal with emergency plumbing catastrophes. The more your responsibilities grow, the more this radius may shrink. Consider Jim, a multifamily property investor. He once invested in a lovely apartment complex that was, unfortunately, a three-hour drive away. When an unforeseen water leakage occurred in one of the units at midnight, he found himself navigating desolate roads instead of catching up on sleep. After that episode, he limited his investments to a much closer perimeter. By being closer to your investments, you can personally monitor and assess them. It simplifies communication with contractors and reduces misunderstandings, similar to ordering coffee in person versus via an app. The takeaway: keep your properties within a comfortable distance to maintain both sanity and efficiency.

In another example of how proximity to investment is beneficial, at a 13-unit 1980s construction property, my property manager informed me that the garage doors were heavy and had run down the motor for one garage. It seemed like multiple garage motors would need to be fixed at the cost of more than $10,000. When I went to the property, I noticed the mechanism pulling the garage door itself was slipping. After confirming the make and model of the garage motor online, I had a new one in my hands just two days later for $14 with free shipping. To this day, it still works. Being present at the property allowed me to spend $14 to save $10,000. I wouldn't have had the time to spend thinking about something that easy if it was an out-of-area property, especially one I would have needed to fly to.

The further you go outside the areas you know, the more risk you are taking. You might be able to buy larger complexes with less money down, but do you truly know the regional governance or expectations that come with the territory? It could be a big learning process to understand seasonal flooding in Austin that locals know could cause damage and should be a built-in expense. Or the local area may have competing properties paying for all utilities even if your building is separately metered, where you may mistakenly think that the residents would pay.

You can still opt to buy properties beyond your immediate periphery. You may even know others who have made sizable returns and gotten to travel great distances in the process, which could be a fun thing to do if you enjoy the process. It ultimately comes down to how you want to spend your time, the trust you are willing to extend to others you work with, and the level of effort and communication you can commit to. I keep my investments manageable by trusting others to make the right choices without me in most cases. It just makes things go along faster.

That being said, even when I trust others, I often get involved so much that it defeats the purpose of delegating. Hence, I've found that to minimize miscommunications and maximize the asset's value, it is best to be present and local frequently on the property.

For example, I walked through a 1920s two-bedroom property I own that has big closets with windows and wasted space in the hallways. I realized after walking through that I could easily convert it to a three-bedroom. This isn't something my vendors and trusted participants would have devised. It was a choice I had to use my own experience, analysis, and intuition to arrive at. I even had to negotiate a bit with my trusted business partner of 20+ years to see the vision to completion.

Many real estate brokers come to me and try to show "investment opportunities" across the country in areas as far away as Tampa, FL, Austin, TX, Columbus, OH, etc. These are all great areas with burgeoning economies.

But home is where the heart is. I strongly recommend and believe that you should not be an owner of a property that you cannot visit within a short drive. If you are a person who likes driving and is willing to know that you may have to make that drive every weekend, then the distance can be moderately subjective. However, if you are anything like me or most likely the next person, you've got many other things you would rather be doing than wasting time driving needlessly. Hence, I don't like to invest in properties that are more than a 20–30 minute drive from where I live. A big reason to have your investment property in such close proximity is to keep your eye on the property and ensure everything functions as it should. I guarantee you that no one will care more about your property's success and proper function than yourself. Also, with this implicit concern, you will be better suited to verify that the work quoted needs to be done, is completed satisfactorily, and there is less puffing by vendors as far as work needed or completed.

The importance of being able to incorporate keeping a close enough eye on your property cannot be reiterated enough. My dad once had a property in California City, which was quite a few hours' drive from where we lived. Every few months, he would want to visit this property or have me visit it, and for one reason or another, the desire and time constraints to go out to this property kept us pushing off the drive. After about one year of not visiting and finally getting around to it, we found out the property had a major fire. The biggest theory was that there were people who had done methamphetamines on the property and accidentally burned it down. It wasn't a positive realization but a sharp reminder that no one will care about your property more than you do.

Across different cities are recurring variables that will make it easier for you to narrow down what areas you'd feel most comfortable investing in. These variables are employment, construction, household quantity, demographics, rental rates, vacancy rates, and income levels. Choosing an area that has consistent employment is a key variable for me. I love having the port nearby in Long Beach and major businesses and institutions such as the Long Beach Unified School District and Long Beach Memorial. The physical proximity between Orange and Los Angeles counties also bodes well for those who choose to live at a midway point between their work in either direction.

BUILDING PERMITS

When identifying potential investment opportunities, one key factor is the number of building permits issued in a specific area. The trend in building permits can provide insight into whether an area faces overbuilding or a housing shortage.

Long Beach, which is the 5th largest city in California, currently has a relatively low number of building permits compared to other areas. This suggests that new construction in Long Beach may be limited and that the city focuses on more creative solutions such as infill development and building existing properties. These types of projects often carry more risk but also have the potential for higher returns. With housing demand outpacing supply in Long Beach, rental rates will likely continue rising. Long Beach's growing population and rising household income make it an attractive location for long-term rental property investments.

Building permits can be useful for investors when assessing the real estate market in a specific area. An investor can gain insight into the housing market's current state, including the supply and demand for new housing, by analyzing the number of building permits issued over time. Here are a few specific ways that building permits can help guide an investor's decisions:

Identifying areas with a shortage of housing: A low number of building permits over a prolonged period can indicate a shortage of housing in the area. When supply is low, demand is high, which can lead to higher rental rates and property values. This can be a good indicator for investors to consider buying properties as rental properties or to hold them as an investment.

Avoiding overbuilt markets: Conversely, a high number of building permits over a prolonged period can indicate an oversupply of housing in the area. In such a case, demand is low, and rental rates and property values are likely to be depressed. This could be a sign for investors to avoid investing in that specific area.

Identifying upcoming construction: Building permits also provide information about upcoming construction projects. By tracking building permits, an investor can identify areas where new housing developments are planned, which can be useful information when assessing future demand and rental rate growth.

Identifying areas where the city is taking creative solutions. As previously mentioned, if an area's building permits are lower than other similar areas and the city is taking creative solutions like building up the property, it will require more sophisticated builders with greater risk/reward scenarios. This may be an opportunity for an experienced investor willing to take on more risk for a potentially higher return.

In the modern age, it's all too easy to outsource most of the property scouting process. You can easily hire people to research opportunities, meet with agents, and take detailed photos and videos for you. But putting your boots on the ground throughout every journey confers unique and valuable advantages. You're not just looking at the properties themselves. You look at everything around the properties that affects how they will be perceived on the market and the general trajectory of the area's future. This is the way to spot opportunities other real estate investors might overlook because they aren't doing the legwork you are. Suppose you can find indicators that a poor or underdeveloped area will soon become more popular with a certain type of person and be gentrified. In that case, you can position yourself now to get in on the ground floor while it's still cheap and be ready to offer your units at higher rents once that trendy new series of shops opens up nearby.

SWEAT EQUITY AREAS

Once you've identified the range in which you are comfortable looking for rental properties, go onto websites for local services like Yelp, Next Door, and Google business profiles and browse for their new and hip restaurants, bars, shops, or social venues in that area. Have you ever found a really good restaurant or coffee shop in a sketchy area? Maybe you love their menu options and will drive out of your way to get there because it is so good. Start with venues like coffee shops in marginal neighborhoods that are really well-rated and look at the neighborhood. Walk around the area. Look for lower-end properties being rented cheaply that could command a much higher rent if they were in better condition and positioned appropriately on the market. These areas are most likely areas in transition that are gentrifying. Many people with good ideas for restaurants, shops, or stores choose to open up shop in neighborhoods where it is significantly cheaper and less desirable. The people who are willing to invest their time and resources in worse neighborhoods must have confidence that they will be able to put in hustle, hard work, and sweat equity to make it work.

The most promising areas are typically the ones getting a lot of attention from a certain type of person who is always looking for opportunities on the cusp of breaking out. In California, we often call them "hipsters." They typically have more than one income, no kids, fewer familial responsibilities, and more free time. A hipster is typically someone in their late 20s to early 40s who has already made their money through the grind. They tend to have a more artistic bent and style, which can be shown in their fashion choices, facial hair, or other uniquely identifying physical factors. They have a certain air about them that is slightly different from the average bear.

You can even see the history of places that reviewers have reviewed. From that, you can see patterns emerging about what kind of people they are. Then, look at the local pricing for the type of real estate you're invested in and see how much cheaper it is compared to more established areas, and you've got an idea of where to be.

THE MARKET CYCLE

The market cycle is a fundamental concept for any real estate investor to understand. It refers to the natural pattern of growth and decline that occurs in real estate markets, and it is comprised of four phases: expansion, peak, contraction, and trough. Understanding the market cycle is essential to successful real estate investing as it can provide valuable insights into the current state of the market and help you identify potential opportunities and risks.

The expansion phase is the first phase of the market cycle. It is characterized by increasing demand for properties, rising property values, and low unemployment rates. This phase is characterized by a shortage of properties, which can lead to increased competition among buyers, bidding wars, and rising property values. This is a great time to invest in real estate as you can take advantage of the rising prices, generate positive cash flow, and potentially benefit from appreciation.

The peak phase is the second phase of the market cycle. It is characterized by a saturation of the market, with supply and demand in balance. Property values have reached their highest point, and the market has reached a state of maturity. This is not a good time to invest as prices are at their highest point, and there are very limited opportunities for appreciation.

The contraction phase is the third phase of the market cycle. It is characterized by decreasing demand for properties, falling property values, and increasing unemployment rates. This phase is characterized by an oversupply of properties, which can lead to increased competition among sellers, declining property values, and difficulty in finding tenants. This is not a good time to invest in real estate as the market is declining.

The trough phase is the fourth phase of the market cycle. It is characterized by a low point in the market, with low demand for properties, low property values, and high unemployment rates. This phase is characterized by a surplus of properties, which can lead to low prices, reduced competition, and high vacancy rates. This is a good time to invest in real estate as properties are often priced at a discount, and there are opportunities for appreciation as the market begins to recover.

It's important to note that the market cycle can vary in length and timing depending on the location and the real estate market conditions. However, by understanding the market cycle, you can identify opportunities and risks in the market and make informed decisions about when to buy and sell properties.

INTEREST RATES

Interest rates play a significant role in real estate investing as they can greatly impact the affordability of properties and the cost of borrowing money. When interest rates are low, it makes it more affordable for buyers to purchase properties, as the cost of borrowing money is less. This can lead to an increase in demand for properties, which can push property values up. Low interest rates also make it more affordable for landlords to borrow money to purchase rental properties, which can increase the potential for rental income. On the other hand, when interest rates are high, it makes it more expensive for buyers to purchase properties and for landlords to borrow money to purchase rental properties, which can decrease the demand for properties and lead to a decline in property values. As a real estate investor, it's important to keep an eye on interest rates and consider how they may impact your potential returns on investment.

KNOWING THE BEST TIME TO BUY

When it comes to real estate investing, timing can be a crucial factor in determining the success of the investment. Real estate markets are constantly fluctuating, and the timing of your investment can greatly impact your potential returns.

In any form of investing, the timing of the market has a big impact on your opportunity to make a profit (or even just prevent a loss). All other things being equal, you want to buy assets when the market conditions favor buyers and sell them when market conditions favor sellers. And certainly, there are plenty of people who make a lot of money in real estate just by buying property when the market is at a record low, waiting for it to appreciate to many times what they paid for it, and then selling and walking away much richer. But the beautiful thing about investing in multi-family rental properties is that you are not dependent solely on market appreciation to create a return for you, which makes the timing of your purchase far more flexible.

My guiding principle is to buy whenever I'm in a good position to buy and I spot an opportunity that matches my investment criteria. You don't need to follow real estate cycles and time the market with impeccable precision in order to get involved in rental properties and leverage your way to a profit. It's more important to pay attention to your own financial position and individual opportunities as they emerge than the overall market. Even if the on-paper value of the property goes down, you can still maintain good cash flow from increasing rental prices so long as the demand for places to live goes up. So long as the rental income is enough to cover the mortgage. And suppose you're operating in an area with very low vacancy rates (even before taking into account how you might improve the property, make it more attractive, and raise the rents). In that case, you can feel very confident about this remaining true.

Furthermore, due to the 3 D's (death, divorce, and destitution), people often sell properties for below market value in areas with lots of value-add potential. Perhaps the property was poorly managed, and the rent is currently below the market rate because of it. In a down economy, this can work to a buyer's advantage because multifamily agents may be less able to sell a property at proforma value, which is the perceived market value of the income-producing property, instead of what is actually being brought in from rent.

Depending on where you live and choose to buy, rental vacancies can be near-zero indefinitely. The turnover between apartments emptying and being filled again can be almost immediate on an ongoing basis. You may not even have to advertise the vacancy because you will have a waiting list of tenants and word of mouth on your side. It's rare to have a business that requires so little of your active management yet can still maintain an indefinite list of customers ready to buy as soon as product becomes available.

Even if the market takes a dip, the income generated by buying in an area with rising rental demand still makes it one of the safest possible vehicles for your money. And if the market causes the value of your property to eventually appreciate at the same time you are generating rental income, so much the better. Location, the specifics of the property you are interested in, and your own financial position matter far more than timing the market perfectly.

I'm extremely fortunate that I first got involved with real estate when I was just 21 years old. I ended up in that position because of the many books I read on the subject and the mindset my family inculcated in me from a young age. I made a lot of mistakes at first, but I now realize that I would have most likely made those same mistakes if I had started when I was 30 or 40 instead. It's a learning curve of understanding that can only be conquered with real experience in the field. And because I got started so young, I learned those difficult lessons much earlier than most real estate investors.

Most likely, you will borrow money to purchase your first property. If you're a normal borrower, you're not going to have too much of a down payment. With this in mind, lenders, appraisers, and inspectors don't want to lend too much money on a piece of real estate that will leave them too upside down if they have to take the property back. Therefore, timing the purchase of the property is not as important as getting yourself into the game and getting life experience and a better awareness of what owning and managing property entails. All of this will make it easier to purchase your next property below market value.

There is no right or wrong time to buy a property. It all depends on how hard you are willing to look to find a deal that works out in your favor. If you expect the process to be unequivocally easy, you are setting yourself up for failure. Though there are certainly times when buyers might be generally favored over sellers in the market (or vice versa), there is always at least the possibility of finding hidden value that isn't being openly advertised to the rest of the buying market.

You're not buying the market. You're buying the individual property (or maybe a second property or third property). Each property is unique in its own valuation versus the overall market. For example, I buy properties below market values regardless of whether the economy is going up or down. I typically like to buy things where I can make at least 30% increase in the value within a year. With that 30%, I tend to get about 50 to 100% returns because I put about 30% down. If I put 30% down and it's 30% below market, and then I bring it back up to market, I will make about 100% of my money.

The entry and exit of a property are inextricably linked for me. Foreseeing the conditions under which I will sell a property in the future is an important part of assessing a deal. In chapter 11, we'll go over exit planning in greater detail, but suffice it to say that it begins with the conditions under which you buy a property and your expectations for the future with it.

I strongly believe in planning for an exit from the start, but I don't always hold fast and firm to my expected exit plan. Sometimes, better opportunities just pop up, and I have to take them. In fact, I've bought properties and sold them in as little as a month. This happened because while I was in escrow, the listing agent who represented me told me another buyer was already interested in taking it off my hands. He also said that he would like to make a commission representing this new buyer. I had just paid $550,000, and we negotiated with the new buyer for a price of $605,000. So, everybody won. I paid my agent his $10,000 commission and walked away about $45,000 richer, not including a few other transactional expenses.

In that situation, if that other buyer hadn't happened to come along and offer me a better price than what I had just paid, I would have kept the property. I would have spent a lot of time and money trying to add value to it, ultimately to sell it at an appreciated price probably about two years later. That was my original exit plan. But since the opportunity for a quick $45,000 happened to come up, I decided it was more in my interest to just take the payday now and invest that money into another property that I could help grow.

When it comes to buying rental real estate, due diligence and market analysis are crucial steps in the process. Due diligence is the process of conducting a thorough investigation of a property before making a purchase. This includes reviewing financial statements, assessing the physical condition of the property, and evaluating the potential risks and liabilities associated with the property. By conducting due diligence, investors can identify potential issues and make informed decisions about whether or not to move forward with a purchase.

Market analysis and forecasting are also important factors to consider when buying rental real estate. This involves analyzing the local real estate market to determine current trends and potential future changes that could impact the value of the property. Investors should look at key indicators such as population growth, job growth, and rental vacancy rates to assess the demand for rental properties in a particular area.

When choosing an area to focus on, investors should consider factors such as proximity to amenities, transportation options, and the quality of the local school district. Additionally, investors should pay attention to building permits in the area, as this can indicate potential growth and development in the area.

Sweat equity areas can also be attractive to investors, as these are areas where properties may be undervalued due to a lack of upkeep or maintenance. Investors who are willing to put in the work to renovate and improve these properties can potentially see a significant return on their investment.

Knowing the best time to buy is another important consideration for investors. Generally, the best time to buy is when prices are low and demand is high. This may require patience and careful monitoring of the market, but can ultimately lead to a better return on investment.

To determine the value of a property, investors can use a variety of methods, such as the income approach, the cost approach, or the sales comparison approach. These methods involve assessing factors such as rental income potential, the cost of construction or renovation, and comparable sales in the area.

Ultimately, conducting due diligence and market analysis are essential steps for any rental real estate investor. By thoroughly evaluating a property and the local market, investors can make informed decisions and maximize their potential return on investment.

CHAPTER 5
VALUING REAL ESTATE FOR YOUR FIRST PURCHASE

"Don't wait to buy real estate. Buy real estate and wait."
—Will Rogers

In real estate, determining a property's value is a bit like finding the sweet spot in a negotiation. Let's imagine a scenario: you are at a yard sale, and you come across a beautiful antique chair that you'd like to take home. The seller, who is also fond of the chair, has tagged it at a higher price than you're willing to pay. In this situation, you might try to negotiate, but if the seller isn't comfortable going as low as your maximum price and you aren't comfortable paying as much as the seller's lowest price, then a sale doesn't occur. This is because there's a disagreement on the chair's value.

Similarly, when selling a property, the seller usually has a minimum price they'd be comfortable accepting, known as the "lowest acceptable selling price." On the flip side, the buyer has a maximum price they'd be willing to pay for the property, or the "highest comfortable purchase price."

The value of the property, then, could be seen as the overlapping area between what the seller is willing to accept and what the buyer is willing to pay. If both parties find a price within that overlap that they're comfortable with, then the property is sold.

However, if the seller's minimum is higher than the buyer's maximum, there's a disagreement about the property's value, and it's unlikely the property will sell unless one or both parties adjust their comfort levels.

So, in layman's terms, the value of a property is essentially the price which a willing seller and a willing buyer agree to transact. If they can't find a mutually agreeable price, then in their eyes, the property's value to each of them remains different. When there's a large number of similar properties, subjective interpretations of their value will diminish. When fewer rental properties on the market cater to a similar class of tenants, their subjective value increases. This is just an application of basic supply and demand.

When it comes to selling a property, several different parties are involved, each with their own goals and priorities. The listing agent, for example, is primarily focused on getting the best possible outcome for the seller and will typically highlight the property's positive features and comparable points that are likely to attract buyers. In contrast, the selling agent who represents the buyer will be more interested in identifying any potential issues or weaknesses with the property that could be used to negotiate a lower price.

Lenders and appraisers also have their own goals and priorities when evaluating a property. Lenders are primarily concerned with assessing the property's value in order to determine how much to lend to the buyer. They will typically be more focused on the property's overall condition and value relative to the loan amount. On the other hand, appraisers are typically focused on providing an independent assessment of the property's value to ensure that the sale price is in line with market conditions.

Despite these different perspectives and priorities, all of these parties are ultimately working together to get the deal done. They may have different agendas and goals, but they all have a vested interest in ensuring that the property is sold and that the transaction is completed smoothly.

HOW INVESTORS ASSESS THE VALUE OF REAL ESTATE

As an investor, you can't really know what makes a purchase a good deal for you unless you understand best how to value a rental property. With real estate, there are three common ways to assess the value of the asset:

The Income Method, also known as the income capitalization approach, is a method used to value a property by considering the potential income it can generate from renting it out. This method is commonly used for valuing rental properties, such as apartments, office buildings, and shopping centers.

The basic principle behind this method is that the value of a property is equal to the present value of its future income. To use this method, the first step is to determine the property's potential rental income. This can be done by researching similar properties in the area and their rental rates or by estimating the income based on the property's size, location, and condition.

Once the potential rental income is determined, the next step is to estimate the property's expenses, such as property taxes, insurance, and maintenance costs. These expenses are subtracted from the potential rental income to determine the property's net operating income (NOI).

The NOI is then used to calculate the property's value. This is typically done by dividing the NOI by a capitalization rate, which is a percentage that represents the rate of return an investor expects from a similar property in the same area.

Net Operating Income (NOI)	Capitalization Rate (Cap Rate)	Property Value
$100,000	8%	$1,250,000

Explanation:

- The property generates a Net Operating Income (NOI) of $100,000 per year.
- The Capitalization Rate (Cap Rate), which is the rate of return expected on the property, is 8%.

- The Property Value, calculated as NOI divided by the Cap Rate (100,000 / 0.08), comes out to be $1,250,000.

This means that if the property is generating $100,000 in profit annually and the expected rate of return is 8%, the estimated value of the property would be $1,250,000.

It's worth mentioning that this method is useful for income-producing properties, where the income generated is enough to cover the costs and generate a profit. Also, it is more common for commercial real estate, for example, an office building with several tenants, as it provides more stability and predictability of the income generated. This method is not as effective for valuing owner-occupied properties, such as single-family homes, as the rental income may not be the main consideration of the property's value. It's also important to note that the Income Method makes the assumption that the property's income and expenses will remain constant over time, which may not always be the case.

The Replacement Cost Method, also known as the cost approach, is a method used to value a property by determining the cost of replicating the property with a similar structure of the same quality, size, and features. This method is primarily used for valuing residential properties, such as single-family homes, and other physical structures like commercial or industrial properties.

To use this method, the first step is to determine the construction cost for a similar property with the same characteristics and features as the subject property. This includes factors such as the size of the property, the type of construction, the materials used, and any unique features. This cost can be estimated by researching the prices of similar properties in the area, consulting with builders and contractors, or using cost-estimating software.

Once the cost of construction has been determined, the next step is to calculate the property's value by factoring in the land value and the depreciation of the building. The land value is determined by researching the prices of similar land in the area, and the depreciation is calculated by subtracting the age and condition of the building from the original cost of construction.

Original Building Cost (20 years ago)	Current Construction Cost (for a comparable home today)	Land Value	Total Replacement Cost	Depreciation Over 20 Years	Estimated Value (After Depreciation)
$200,000	$400,000	$150,000	$550,000	$100,000	$450,000

Explanation:

- The home was originally built 20 years ago at a cost of $200,000.
- To build a similar home today would cost $400,000.
- The value of the land on which the home is built is $150,000.
- Thus, the total replacement cost (current construction cost + land value) is $550,000.
- Given that the building has depreciated over the past 20 years, we subtract the depreciation of $100,000.
- Therefore, the estimated current value of the home (after considering depreciation) would be $450,000.

The Replacement Cost Method assumes you can recreate a property with current costs. However, this doesn't apply to all properties. Consider historic buildings like the Notre Dame Cathedral. Its unique architecture, historical value, and antique materials can't be simply replaced or replicated at today's costs, making the Replacement Cost Method less relevant.

The Comparable Sales Method, also known as the market approach, is a method used to value a property by comparing it to similar properties that have recently sold in the same area. This method is commonly used for valuing residential and commercial properties such as single-family homes, apartments, and office buildings.

To use this method, the first step is to identify comparable properties that have recently sold in the same area and that have similar characteristics to the subject property. These characteristics include factors such as the size of the property, the number of bedrooms and bathrooms, the age and condition of the property, and any unique features. This information can be obtained through public records, real estate databases, or by working with a real estate professional.

Once comparable properties have been identified, the next step is to analyze the sales data to determine the value of the subject property. This typically involves comparing the sale prices of the comparable properties to the subject property, adjusting for any differences in the characteristics of the properties. Some of the common inputs used with this method in multi-family real estate include the cost of the building, the cost per square foot of the land, the cost per unit, and the income from the rental units.

Comparable Property A	Comparable Property B	Subject Property
$500,000	$450,000	Between $450,000 and $500,000

Explanation:

- Comparable Property A sold for $500,000
- Comparable Property B sold for $450,000
- Given that the Subject Property is larger than both A and B, its value would fall somewhere between $450,000 and $500,000, likely closer to $500,000 due to its larger size.

The Comparable Sales Method, based on the premise that similar properties in the same vicinity will share comparable values, isn't always foolproof. It's crucial to meticulously identify comparable properties and account for unique traits of the property under consideration that might affect its value. The evaluation of comparables goes beyond mere similarity; it requires a deep understanding of the variables that could potentially influence value.

Imagine you own a duplex in Long Beach's Belmont Shore neighborhood. You're looking to value it using the Comparable Sales Method, so you find another duplex that recently sold in the same area.

Though both properties share similar features - like the number of units and rooms - your duplex is closer to the beach with ocean views, a coveted feature. The other property, though similar in structure, doesn't have this advantage as it's further inland.

In essence, despite the structural similarities, the proximity to the beach and the ocean view significantly raise the value of your duplex. Therefore, in the Comparable Sales Method, it's not just about structural likeness; unique attributes, like location and views, play a crucial role in property valuation.

APPRAISAL

An appraisal is when you hire a third-party individual to give their professional determination of what the value of a property will be. The appraised value of the property can end up being significantly higher or lower than what you are willing to buy the property for. If you're borrowing the money to be able to buy the property, you may need to come up with more money down to cover the shortfall on the appraisal.

If you don't want to pay for an appraiser, another option is a broker option of value (BOV) or broker price opinion (BPO). It involves an expert in the field, usually a real estate broker, who deals with properties on a daily basis, giving an informal breakdown of what they think the value of the property is.

An appraisal is a process of hiring a professional, known as an appraiser, to determine the value of a property. The appraised value is the expert's professional opinion of the worth of the property. It is important to note that the appraised value may not be the same as the purchase price or the value the buyer is willing to pay for the property. If the buyer is financing the purchase, they may need to come up with additional funds to make up the difference between the appraised value and the purchase price.

When purchasing a property, it's important to note that the appraisal process typically comes after due diligence, which is the investigation of the property and any other relevant information, and before the removal of contingencies, which are the conditions that must be met for the sale to go through. Sometimes appraisals may not come before certain contingencies are removed, as they can be numerous, varied, or even run in conjunction. They allow investors to back out of a deal if they aren't fulfilled.

If the bank can get the property valued at less, they have less risk, so there could appear to be a bias in their appraisal. The bank working with the appraiser gives certain specifications, such as the vacancy factor, which means how much of the property is tenantless throughout the year. Vacancy can fluctuate greatly. It can be 3%. It can be 5%. It can be greater. If it's a ten-unit property and one unit is vacant, that's already a 10% vacancy factor.

Real estate agents typically use a 3% vacancy factor over a year to appraise a property's value. That low figure increases the expected net operating income. However, the bank wants to use a higher vacancy rate in their appraisals, such as 5% or greater, because that decreases the gross effective income and, subsequently, the net operating income. The value of a property is based on the income it drives, and the bank typically prefers greater collateral to mitigate risk and, by default, a lower loan-to-value ratio. This shouldn't be perceived as negative, as banks are a sign of stability and are needed to help keep an economy going. Just think of how chaotic our world was when Lehman Brothers and Bear Stearns went under.

It's crucial to stress that with the insights and strategies provided in this book, readers can arm themselves with the knowledge to weather all sorts of financial storms. Just as some investors persevered and even thrived during the turmoil that followed the 2008 financial crisis, readers of this book are equipped to navigate through market complexities and unpredictabilities. The goal is not merely to survive but to thrive in any investment climate.

Banks can also mitigate risk on other items, like the debt service coverage ratio and the debt coverage ratio. This is typically a number between one and 1.5, depending on the risk tolerance.

Net Operating Income (NOI) for a Year	Debt Service Coverage Ratio (DSCR)	Loan Repayment Annually	Loan Repayment Monthly
$150,000	1.5	$100,000	$8,333

Explanation:

- The Net Operating Income (NOI) for a year is $150,000.
- The Debt Service Coverage Ratio (DSCR), which is a measure of risk tolerance, is set at 1.5.
- By dividing the NOI by the DSCR (150,000 / 1.5), we get $100,000. This is the amount that can be dedicated to loan repayment per year.

- To determine the monthly loan repayment amount, we divide this annual repayment by 12 (100,000 / 12), resulting in approximately $8,333 per month. This represents the maximum amount a loan can be, based on the current NOI and DSCR.

Another tool that banks can use is operating expenses. Typically, for a multi-family property, the operating expenses are anywhere between 20% and 40% of the property. If you have a property that's really locked in and has low expenses because you've put the utility bills onto the tenants to pay, you don't need a gardener because you used drought tolerant plants, and you have solar and all these other things, it still may not matter. The bank has a common metric to determine what the property should have based on general operating practices. They could pump up the apparent operating expenses to lower the net operating income and the value of the property to protect their interests.

Going into a purchase, I was once told that I could buy an 18-unit apartment building with a loan. The purchase price was $1,000,000, and I thought I would only have to put $300,000 down. Then in the 11th hour, the appraisal came back with a much higher figure that suddenly required me to put down twice as much as I had anticipated. Because of that, I had to use money I had saved for another building.

Because of the higher appraisal amount, I needed to bring in a 50% partner to cover the down payment. I ended up going in with my friend Brian at half ownership. We bought the building for $665,000. In just 11 months, we sold it for $1.25 million. Brian was there at the right place at the right time and had the wherewithal and intelligence to pull the trigger. If he hadn't invested, a lot of gains would have been unrealized.

SUBJECTIVITY OF VALUE

The subjectivity of valuation in real estate refers to the fact that there is no one set of objective criteria that can be used to determine the value of a property. Instead, the value of a property is determined based on the subjective opinions and perspectives of those involved in the process, including buyers, sellers, and appraisers.

There are many different factors that can contribute to the subjectivity of valuation in real estate. These can include the property's location, condition, features, and potential for appreciation. For example, a property in a desirable neighborhood with good schools and amenities may be considered more valuable than a similar property in a less desirable area. Similarly, a property in good condition with modern finishes and updates may be considered more valuable than a similar property in need of repairs or upgrades.

Other factors that can contribute to the subjectivity of valuation include market conditions, such as the overall demand for real estate in a particular area and the investor's personal preferences and goals. For example, an investor who is looking for a property to flip for a quick profit may place a higher value on a property with the potential for rapid appreciation. In comparison, an investor who is looking for a long-term rental property may place a higher value on a property with the potential for stable, consistent cash flow.

Unlike the stock market, which is heavily influenced by market makers and large numbers of buyers and sellers, real estate transactions involve just one buyer and one seller. This means that, with the right strategy and persistence, an investor can find properties at the price they are willing to pay. Long Beach is one specific area where I've found success as a real estate investor, and I believe others can too. The key is to keep looking and making offers on properties until you find one that works for your investment goals.

Each real estate deal can be very distinct, even when you try to look for commonalities. Further, during the holding period of the property, there could be differences in the operations of the building. One building may be master metered, meaning that the owner pays for all of the electricity. Now you have a tenant who's paying a thousand dollars each month but has all their electricity, gas, water, sewage, and refuse paid by the owner. The average tenant doesn't do the due diligence to understand what the load would be for their electric bill, gas bill, or trash bill. All that they think about is, "This apartment rents for a thousand dollars a month. That's a great deal."

APPRAISAL CONTINGENCY

Exercise caution when adding too many contingencies to the contract in a hot seller's market. However, it's worth noting that an appraisal contingency is a standard clause in commercial real estate contracts, and whether to include it or waive it depends on the local market conditions. An appraisal contingency protects the buyer if the property's appraisal comes in below the agreed-upon sale price. If this happens, the contingency enables the buyer to cancel the contract without having to pay the shortfall out of pocket.

In a hot seller's market, waiving the appraisal contingency may be necessary to make your offer more appealing, especially if bidding wars are common. Conversely, in a buyer's market, appraisal contingencies become more common. It's crucial to differentiate between appraisal contingencies and loan contingencies.

After signing the contract, completing the appraisal contingency typically takes around two to four weeks. The buyer usually pays for the appraisal, which is part of the closing costs with the lender.

Deciding to waive an appraisal contingency should be based on market conditions and your financial situation. While securing a multifamily commercial property in a hot seller's market may be necessary, waiving the appraisal can be risky if you're not prepared to come up with additional funds to satisfy the mortgage lender. Understanding how appraisal contingencies work is essential whether you're buying or selling your property.

DUE DILIGENCE

Negotiating a sale in the current market can be tricky, so it's important to be cautious. Buyers often have a limited idea of what they're willing to pay, which means they'll need a due diligence period to investigate the property further.

During the due diligence period (typically 30–90 days), buyers can inspect the property for any issues, review leases, and make sure their plans for the property make financial sense. But as the period comes to a close, the seller may receive a request for an extension or a price reduction. To avoid the property being perceived as "damaged goods," sellers often accommodate buyers to some extent.

The parties may agree on specific conditions if the buyer requests an extension. However, a request for a price adjustment creates more complications for the seller. They may offer to accelerate the closing or increase the deposit, but demanding future payments based on the property's performance is unlikely to work. To protect themselves, sellers can charge a non-refundable option fee or create a contract that allows the buyer to terminate only if they identify significant problems with the property.

To mitigate the effect of generous due diligence periods in contracts, sellers should time their sales to occur during a seller-friendly market. If that's not possible, the contract could build in the possibility of an extension fee if the buyer wants more time. Additionally, the seller should not agree to exclusivity with any buyer and make it clear that they have the right to negotiate and sign backup contracts with other potential buyers. By understanding these dynamics, investors can make better decisions when negotiating commercial real estate contracts.

UNIT INSPECTIONS

Suppose you're walking through a property and see obvious problems like black mold, subflooring under a toilet caving, or six appliances plugged into the same electrical outlet. These are all signs of neglect or deferred maintenance. Always get the right inspector or general contractor to determine all the possible problems with the property and what they will cost to fix. Someone who is not an expert in the field is not going to know the building codes or the recent supply chain issues for the necessary materials.

I've had many deals where inspectors come back with between $10,000 and $400,000 in estimated future repair costs. When I bring this to the seller's attention, they either ignore it or concede somewhat on the price they were previously negotiating with me. Sometimes, they cover it all, and sometimes, we meet somewhere in the middle. Regardless, you've got to be informed that you could be buying a property that has not been handled properly and that you're going to be facing these problems as its new owner.

I often get great deals on neglected properties, or what I call "Ugly Betties." I love them because my cost of bringing the property up to a livable condition is usually far lower than what the old owner would have had to pay. This is because, through the years, I've found the right contractors or tradesmen to do the right job for the right price at sufficient volume. The more you're in the game, the more you will build these relationships. You will have more of a competitive advantage against other owners who don't put as much thought and effort into these things.

CONTRACTOR QUOTES

Accompanying proper inspection should be contractor's quotes. Sometimes, they can come in severely high compared to the picture the owner painted for you. Why are the staircase and railing going to cost $30,000? Oh, because the sub-lining is flooded. They need to go in and remove the wood, and it turns out this type of wood is no longer for sale. We need to bring everything up to code.

Of course, you don't have to do everything the way a professional suggests. Maybe there's a cheaper way that will last for only five years instead of 50. That's at your discretion, but you at least need to know the range of prices and possibilities, and everything's subject to interpretation. You can have two super experienced, knowledgeable, and intelligent contractors give you different information and opinions.

The more information you get, the more leverage you have in negotiations with the seller. If you are in escrow and you notify the seller of deferred maintenance problems, under California law, they have to inform other buyers, too. This increases your bargaining power because you are lowering the appeal of the property in the eyes of your competition. You are building a paper trail to substantiate your position and legitimately negotiate a concession or a lower amount on the price.

MARKET ANALYSIS

Suppose you look at the going rate of a one-bedroom apartment of a particular size in a particular area with particular amenities. In that case, you can argue the price of the property you want to buy based on that data set. You have to have a sound understanding of what the rent should be and what the comparables are to make an informed decision. Don't just look at rents in the area. Look at how the properties are operated and what's been done to improve them. What is the effective life of the roof? What are the upgrades to the property? Are the units separately metered? Is there free Wi-Fi?

They're so many different considerations to take into play. As a result, most people aren't able to do a sound market survey. They have to go off of certain assumptions. All of this is a product of time, energy, and experience, so the more you do it, even if you're not buying, the more knowledgeable you become and the better you become at it.

COMPETITOR ANALYSIS

It's obviously to your advantage to know what competitors are selling for, the cap rates, the GRMs, the prices per unit, and more. Seek to know as much relevant info as you can. Knowledge is power. You've got to be able to determine what a buyer is going to be looking at. Why are they going to be buying your property over another property? What benefits do you bring to the property that are greater than what someone else brings? This is why it may work to your advantage to find something that helps to improve the property that other people don't do. For example: providing free Wi-Fi, putting solar panels on the roof, or other elements covered in Chapter 8. All these value-add improvements can help you to differentiate in some way.

ENVIRONMENTAL PHASE ONE

Suppose there used to be a gas station on an apartment building's land. That could end up being a major environmental problem. That's why you want to look at the environmental inspection report. Are you in an area where there's a Coastal Commission? What about a historical zone where advocates want to maintain the beauty, joy, and luster of properties? This means everything is required to look the same within certain tolerable limits. So now you have to go find a specialist who knows how to do that. Naturally, costs go up, and profits go down.

There was a project called the Sea Port Marina motel getting built along the Pacific Coast Highway in Southern California. They had to do an environmental impact report about how the traffic would be with all the cars going in and out. That delayed construction and cost the owner a lot of their leverage. This could have been avoided with the right environmental inspection report.

Are you building on a hill? That hill might be caving in. You could be on expansive soil, which means it won't be stable. You have to do soil reports and make sure that you have the property on sound land. The billion-dollar skyscrapers in San Francisco are sinking two inches per year because the soil is not sound. This is a huge insurance cost and caring cost.

DEMOGRAPHICS

It's important to pay attention to demographics so that you can buy primarily where local indicators of stability exist, such as easy access to employment and modern social amenities. It's usually easy to get a general sense if a local area is on its way up or out by the type of people coming in or leaving, how they are putting down roots and spending their money, etc. Are people comfortable and happy there? Or are most people looking for an opportunity to leave? Are young creative people moving in and setting up shop?

Pay attention to other important variables already covered, such as the level of new residential real estate construction (as determined by active building permits in a given area), how much existing units rent for, and the overall vacancy rate. What's the local employment situation like? I consider that one of the most important factors. And remember: With higher income comes the ability to pay higher rents.

PENDING LITIGATION

At any point, a property could have pending litigation, known legally as a lis pendens notice. This means that a lean is pending. It's a way that attorneys can delay a sale or notify any potential buyers that there could be an impending cloud on title. That could be, for example, if somebody executes a long-term lease for a laundry company and the seller does not notify you of it. You now have a cloud on the title. You either have to accept it, or you don't. If you don't, you go back to the seller and inform them they did not disclose it and that it affects the value of the property.

In a 20-unit apartment building I wanted to buy, I discovered at the last minute that they had an oil royalty on the property. This, understandably, annoyed me. I had negotiated in good faith with the seller to bring down their initial asking price of $2.1 million to $1.67 million. When I brought the oversight to their attention, they claimed that they didn't bother to mention it because it was not a lot of money—only $200,000 to $300,000 a year. These are things that have to be clearly disclosed and understood from the onset.

DELINQUENCIES

If a seller claims that all units have been paying their rent, and that's not exactly true, it means they're misrepresenting the cash flow of the property and the ease of management. This is why you have the due diligence period to cover yourself.

Or perhaps there are undisclosed family members living on the property. I once bought a property where a family friend of the previous owner was the on-site manager. He was living rent-free in a unit that was not up to code. After several bad experiences with him as my manager, I asked him to leave. Well, he wasn't very receptive to that request, so I had to evict him. During the eviction, he complained to the city that the unit he was living in was not actually on the title. I had to have the unit closed off and made inoperable, which finally got him to leave. Now, I'm finally in a position where I can re-open the unit again and bring it up to code to make it rentable to new tenants.

CAPITALIZATION RATE

The capitalization rate, or cap rate, is a commonly used metric in commercial real estate to determine the profitability of a property. It is calculated by dividing the property's market value by the net operating income (NOI), which is the income left after operating expenses are subtracted from gross operating revenue.

For example, a property with a $5 million market value and an annual NOI of $250,000 has a cap rate of 5%. This means the property would generate 5% of the purchase price annually. The cap rate can be affected by various factors, including interest rates, relative valuation, property condition, and any extra perks or opportunities for improvement. Higher interest rates may lead to higher cap rates due to increased risk, while lower interest rates may result in lower cap rates. The cap rate of a property may also be influenced by the cap rates of similar properties in the area. The condition of the property, as well as any potential for improvement or increased income, can also affect the cap rate.

METHODS FOR CALCULATING CAP RATE

The three most common methods for calculating cap rate are the build-up method, the market extraction method, and the band-of-investment method.

The build-up method combines various factors such as interest rates, liquidity premiums, recapture premiums, and risk premiums to determine the cap rate. It can be accurate, but it is only as accurate as the source of the data used.

The market extraction method uses historical sales data and other relevant valuation figures to determine the cap rate. It involves averaging the cap rates of similar properties in the area to find the appropriate rate for a particular deal.

The band-of-investment method is particularly suitable for financed deals, as it takes into account debt and equity financing. It calculates the cost of capital needed to finance a deal and can be customized based on the specifics of the financing arrangement.

INTERNAL RATE OF RETURN

The Internal Rate of Return (IRR) is a method of evaluating real estate investments that considers the current economic environment and potential future economic conditions. This method is often preferred by advanced investors, particularly institutions, because it allows for more accurate forecasting and risk management. The IRR is determined by finding the discount rate that results in the Net Present Value (NPV) of the investment's cash flow being equal to zero. This means that the IRR takes into account changes in economic variables over time and accounts for the possibility that the investment's cash flow may lose value in the future. The IRR is a more detailed approach that aims to mitigate risks and uncertainties in the future.

IRR VS. CAP RATE

The internal rate of return is a financial measure that helps investors evaluate the potential profitability of a real estate investment. It is calculated by determining the discount rate that will make the **net present value (NPV)** of the investment equal to zero. The NPV considers all projected cash flows, including expected operating expenses, capital expenses (such as loan payments and loan payoffs), and projected sales proceeds.

The IRR is often compared to the **capitalization rate** (cap rate), which is a measure of the potential rate of return on a real estate investment. However, the IRR is generally considered to be a more conservative measure because it takes into account potential risks and uncertainties and assumes that the property will eventually be sold in order to recover the investment and make a profit. This makes the IRR a popular tool among advanced investors and institutions.

In addition to comparing the IRR to the cap rate, investors may also use the IRR to compare real estate investments to other investment vehicles, such as stocks and private equity. This is because the IRR is a time-weighted return measure, similar to other metrics used to evaluate the performance of these assets. This allows commercial investors, particularly passive limited partners with diversified portfolios, to set cash flow expectations and determine the yields on their investments.

KEY VARIABLES OF INTERNAL RATE OF RETURN

Inflation is an important factor to consider when calculating an investment's internal rate of return. As the value of money decreases over time, it is important for an investment to generate a certain level of returns in order to maintain its value. The IRR takes this into account by using a time-weighted approach, which calculates the value of cash flow over time and adjusts for inflation. This helps investors determine how quickly they can expect to see returns on their investment.

Cash-on-cash return is a way to measure the potential rate of return on a rental property investment. It calculates the net cash flow from the property (after operating expenses and costs of capital) divided by the equity invested. This helps investors understand how long it will take to recover their equity. Cash-on-cash return can be calculated annually or for the entire investment period. It does not factor in proceeds from refinancing or sales, only normal operations. This makes it a useful tool for investors looking for a realistic projection of dividend yields from a rental property.

The **equity multiple** is a measure of the profitability of a rental property, calculated by dividing the total profits by the total equity invested. It provides a rough assessment of a deal's potential returns, taking into account the present value of variables such as cash flow and sales proceeds. In comparison, the internal rate of return is a more specific measure that accounts for the time value of money and other variables and is often used by commercial investors. On the other hand, the cash-on-cash return is an annualized measure of the return on investment, calculated in percentage terms. While the equity multiple spans the lifetime of a deal, the cash-on-cash return is typically calculated on an annual basis.

CHAPTER 6
CRITICAL ASPECTS OF A FIRST PURCHASE

"Rule No. 1: Never lose money. Rule No. 2:
Never forget rule No. 1."
—Warren Buffet

This chapter will delve into the crucial aspects of making your first real estate purchase. We will discuss interacting with the seller, understanding the property from the seller's perspective, the purchase process, and negotiating the price and terms of a property. As you embark on your real estate investment journey, it is important to keep in mind that residential and commercial properties require different financing strategies.

When purchasing one-to-four-unit properties, you will primarily deal with residential financing. However, the financing process will change as you transition into commercial or multifamily properties. It is also essential to be aware of alternative financing methods for projects like Accessory Dwelling Units (ADUs) and adaptive reuse projects. As you gain experience and expand your portfolio, you will likely encounter various financing options suitable for your investment strategy.

One of the key aspects of successful real estate investing is recognizing the potential in properties that others might overlook. Properties with deferred maintenance, foundation issues, structural problems, or problem tenants may deter the average investor, but with a higher risk tolerance and a willingness to roll up your sleeves, you could uncover hidden gems with great returns.

For instance, taking on a property with foundation issues or structural problems might involve extra work and unknowns, but the potential payoff can be substantial if you're willing to take on the challenge. Similarly, dealing with problem tenants or managing properties with deferred maintenance can be a lucrative opportunity for investors who are willing to put in the time and effort to resolve these issues. As your risk tolerance and willingness to tackle complex projects grow, you can venture into these commonly undesirable characteristics for potentially greater return.

Investing in rental properties is not for the faint of heart. It requires boldness and a "go big or go home" mentality. However, the decision ultimately depends on the investor's temperament. It is often said that nothing ventured, nothing gained. In terms of diversification, more units are better because it means less reliance on rent from any single unit. For example, a 4-unit property with one vacancy means that 25% of the property is not generating income. This is a bigger concern than a 10-unit property with one vacant unit, which represents only 10% of the property's total rental income.

However, smaller units have their own challenges, such as greater tenant turnover and higher maintenance costs due to frequent touch-ups. The best property for an investor will depend on their objectives, such as their budget and how many units they can afford. While smaller properties with fewer units may seem more budget-friendly, they offer fewer economies of scale, resulting in relatively higher operating costs. It's better to opt for more units if possible because they provide more diversification and economies of scale, mitigating the risk of lost income due to vacancies. Buying even more units and receiving more passive income in a lucrative positive feedback loop becomes easier as an investor acquires more units.

Look at what additional benefits you get by having high-quality common areas, such as laundry, parking, wi-fi, a gym, or outdoor areas. There are a lot of intangible variables that increase quality of life that are not typically found on a report or that a real estate agent wouldn't necessarily know to look for.

How does the sunlight hit the properties? What time of day is the inspection? Do residents leave their items in common areas? Is mail accruing in the mailbox area showing that previous tenants moved on? How well-kept is the landscaping? Is there any paint peeling on the walls? Any watermarks on the property showing where the rain gutters are not working? Are the exterior windows clean and squeegeed, or do they show watermarks? Are the windows themselves showing dust or termite droppings? How current are the vents?

This is an important aspect of personally walking through and investigating every property you are considering buying. There are just too many things you might not think to ask about that could be important to your decision. You've got to shop around and get to know your market. Get to know the properties and the unique amenities, facets, and facilities for each particular property. Then, get an idea of the improvements around the neighborhood, whether you have a Costco or a Walmart or whether you have a good coffee shop. Then, find out how long those positive features have been there. You don't want to buy something based on proximity to some good coffee and then find out that they went under soon after. This way, you will build a foundation from the bottom up. By getting to know the good restaurants, coffee shops, or other local amenities, you'll know when something else across the street is offering a much more attractive environment for renters at the same price (even if its physical condition might require more work).

Another approach is to scour the MLS and real estate portals. The county assessor's office can compile lists for you, or others can sell you lists. I buy my lists primarily from South Bay Directories. Make a social media account advertising that you are looking to invest in properties in your area so prospective sellers should contact you. Hire a company like printlabelmail.com to send out direct mail postcards to property owners in your area.

Do whatever you can to tie up the deal because then you're in the driver's seat. You can ultimately let the deal go, assign the rights to the deal to someone else, or buy the deal. If later, during your physical inspections, you find that the condition is not what you thought, you can always go back to the seller and ask for some kind of credit to cover the difference between what was presented and what it turned out to be.

There are some particular elements to look out for when purchasing a property. Seeing lots of "For Rent" signs or vacancies at a property indicates that there's lots of upside potential from improving the property to make it operate closer to its full capacity. Or the same can be true even if all units are full but are being rented at severely below-market rates. Buildings that look beat up and worn down have obvious potential for renovation. These types of properties will most likely have fed-up owners and/or struggling property management companies behind them.

An eviction is a pain in the butt and one of the last things a building owner wants. When that day comes in court, it's aggravating for both residents and owners. What better place is there to find an underperforming property than in the eviction courtroom when an owner is least happy with their steward-ship? This could be one of the best places to find properties below market value.

FINDING THE RIGHT AGENT OR BROKER FOR A PROPERTY

Real estate agents are the best thing on the planet for real estate investors because they help you find properties you don't know about. They spend time parsing through thousands upon thousands of sources of information, so you don't have to. They talk to people, building rapport and relationships, trying to get the sale. They put in so much time and work to get a property to sell that they're worth every damn penny. However, if you are young, hard-working, and enterprising, you can do much of the work of a real estate agent yourself and get a better price on the purchase.

Be forewarned that most people are not equipped to do the job as well as a professional, though. Many of the best agents in multifamily come from D1 schools and have a background in athletics. These ones survive because discipline and competition were instilled into them by their coaches and ex-perience in sports. Hence, they really enjoy what they do. They are hungry for it. I know more than one former professional athlete turned commercial property agent.

Knowing which real estate agent you will get the most value from isn't always straightforward. You can find an agent that spends years or decades building a relationship with a seller, only to have some new agent who says the right word, knows the right thing, or is from the same town who gets the deal. Though I do work with some key agents over and over again, every time I get a call from a newbie, I give them a chance to demonstrate their value. I ask them, "How long have you been in this? Where'd you go to school? How's the market? What's the best info you've gotten, and what's the worst? How are the sellers feeling?" These real estate agents have boots on the ground. They are the infantry on the frontlines in a war. They are the first people in, and they have the most information. Most importantly, with real estate agents and all people you come in contact with, to get respect, you've got to give respect. We're on this little planet together, and the moment we don't take the time to interact with or at least be respectful to one another, perspective is lost.

Of course, working with real estate agents you have built relationships with is good. But you can't have that be your only way to do real estate. If another agent has the listing and the seller prefers to have the listing agent represent both the buyer and the seller, you're automatically cut off.

Failing to perform is another way to immediately lose any credibility and relationships formed. If you remove contingencies and complete due diligence but can't close, it becomes clear you are not someone who gets things done or keeps their promises. Agents are working to earn a commission and need to make a living. Don't waste their time if you're not prepared to fulfill your agreements.

There are two different types of agents. Listing agents are the ones who like to go after sellers. Buying agents are the ones who like to represent buyers. In some states like California, there's something called dual agency, which means that the real estate agent can represent both the buyer and the seller without a conflict of interest. However, it can be hard to clarify what is a conflict of interest or not because if an agent could be making almost as much as double on the real estate commission with the buyer and seller, they may be more motivated to make it work. That's a two-edged sword because if the agent's financial risk is to lose twice the commission, they may accidentally reveal inside information about the buyer's or seller's motivations just to get the deal done.

A good real estate agent should be able to accurately evaluate what properties are worth on the market. They should be able to highlight and show off the most attractive features of a property, such as its amenities, location, and quality of tenants. The best agent is used to dealing with the difficult problems that can arise with real estate, and they become lifesavers for you when you otherwise would have no idea what to do. A bad real estate agent, on the other hand, will fail to show off and explain everything that makes a property valuable.

GETTING THE CHEESE FOR YOUR FIRST DEAL

For many people, one of the most intimidating things about becoming a real estate investor is the huge up-front investment required for it. Some don't like to spend money they don't already have. Others don't know the first thing about how to go about securing funding from the bank.

A certain peace of mind comes with never going into debt or borrowing money. Investing other people's money involves the risk of managing greater uncertainties. Successful investors deal with uncertainty and the unknown better than most people. The successful real estate investor gets a far higher return on their equity. They have money working for them versus having to work for money. This is where we get the term "leverage" from, where you can get far higher cash-on-cash returns.

If you build a relationship with a seller, you can convince them to lend you the money. Then, seller financing is the best way to go because you're not affecting a relationship with a family member, and you're not having to beg, borrow, or need from others. If you have put your money into an IRA, you will get taxed on it when you want to pull it out. Then you're stuck having your money in the market. However, many people include clauses in those retirement accounts that allow them to buy a home with that money.

If you don't have good credit, your first priority needs to be fixing it. How do you do that? Many websites like Credit Karma offer credit improvement services. You must find a way to pay down your debt. Get some Visas and Mastercards. Get as many cards as you can as young as possible. If you have more than one, you'll be able to improve your credit rating faster. You'll build a much deeper credit history by having more accounts for a longer period of time.

If you're just starting out, you can become an authorized user on a parent's card that has a high credit limit. You can even do the same with an older sibling or family friend. This connects you to them and helps you establish credit. Without credit, you can't buy real estate. Plain and simple. You can through seller financing, but it's much more difficult. You'll have to convince people to lend you money, and they, too, might want to look at your credit history and use that as a criteria for lending to you. At the end of the day, you need credit.

And you've got to stay on good terms with banks. Otherwise, they could blacklist you and choose not to loan to you. Then you're effectively dead in the water. Do not bite the hand that feeds you. Lenders are your best friends because they give you leverage through good debt, which helps you make sizable returns on your money.

It's vital at this stage to be mindful of how you spend the cash you have available. Basic bootstrapping principles apply here. Don't make the mistake of splurging on everything under the sun that could conceivably improve the value of your first property. In fact, do the opposite for now: Do everything within your power to cut costs and expenditures. The same applies to your commercial and management expenses, such as the office space you might rent for yourself and/or your team. Can you afford to quit your normal job at this stage? Or would it be wise to hold onto the salary you are used to for now?

If you're in a pinch and need to determine which bills to pay, focus on the bills that may affect your credit first. Pay off your credit card before your heating bill if you have to, and double up on blankets. Of course, that's easy for me to say because I live in Southern California. Your priorities may be different if you're somewhere cold. The point of this example is to demonstrate the importance of making strategic decisions to keep your credit as pristine as possible. Without great credit, you're less likely to be able to buy real estate. It limits your options.

There are many different ways to get into the game. If buying an apartment building from the get-go seems like too much of a leap, you can start with a condominium or house, fix it up, and flip it. As a matter of fact, people who ultimately end up with apartment buildings often start with some other type of real estate, most often residential.

Crowdsourcing is a good way of raising funds or resources for a project or venture by soliciting contributions from a large number of unrelated people, typically through the internet. In the context of real estate investing, crowdsourcing can be a useful tool for investors to raise the capital needed to purchase or renovate a property.

Several platforms allow investors to solicit investments from the crowd in exchange for a stake in the property or a share of the profits. These platforms typically require investors to create a pitch or presentation detailing the investment opportunity, including information about the property, the planned renovations or improvements, and the expected returns.

Investors can then share this pitch with their network or promote it on social media or other platforms in order to attract investors. Investors can also use these platforms to communicate with other potential investors, answer questions, and provide updates on the progress of the project.

Crowdsourcing can be useful for investors to access capital that may not be available through traditional sources, such as banks or private lenders. However, it's important for investors to carefully consider the risks and rewards of crowdsourcing and to carefully review the terms and conditions of any crowdsourcing platform before committing to an investment.

You can also consider a master lease option to purchase, a type of real estate investment strategy in which an investor leases a property with the option to purchase it later. Under this arrangement, the investor pays rent to the property owner and has the right to purchase the property at a predetermined price and within a certain timeframe.

The investor may also have the option to sublease the property to a tenant to generate rental income and potentially build equity in the property. Suppose the investor chooses to exercise the option to purchase. In that case, they may be able to use the rental income and any appreciation in the value of the property to help finance the purchase.

HOW TO GET MULTIFAMILY LOANS

Multifamily loans are a type of commercial mortgage used to finance properties with five or more units, such as apartments, mixed-use buildings, and smaller buildings like duplexes. These loans can be used to purchase or refinance a property, but the terms and requirements vary widely.

To secure a multifamily loan, it is important to shop around and compare quotes from multiple lenders, considering factors such as the loan amount, interest rates, property cash flow, and personal finances. The loan application process typically involves submitting a letter of intent, application package, and third-party reports, and obtaining preliminary title reports, title insurance, and loan payoff documents. The lender may also request additional items before underwriting the loan, such as estoppels from tenants. Once the loan is approved and signed, the lender will fund the account.

The feasibility of repaying a multifamily loan is often determined using the Debt Service Coverage Ratio (DSCR), which is based on the property's projected rental income and expenses rather than the borrower's personal income. For example, if the expected net rental income is $1,000 per month, the loan amount may not exceed $1,300 (1.3x $1,000).

TYPES OF MULTIFAMILY LENDERS

Multifamily lenders can be classified into four main categories:

- Agency lenders, such as Fannie Mae and Freddie Mac, which provide easy access to capital for affordable housing and make up 50% of the multifamily debt market.
- Bankers, including commercial banks, credit unions, and cooperatives, which make up 28% of the market and offer loans ranging from $500,000 to $100 million with fixed rate terms of 3–7 years.
- Insurance companies, which make up about 10% of the market and offer lower rates and long-term fixed rates but generally prefer larger loans.
- Conduits, mainly investment banks, which make up 3% of the market and offer larger loans above $100 million, using their capital market expertise.

- Outliers, including government programs and investment funds, make up the remaining 9% of the market.

HOW TO CHOOSE THE RIGHT MULTIFAMILY LENDER

After deciding on the type of multifamily lender that best suits you, the next thing is narrowing down your list of potential entities. Narrowing down your sources is usually the same whether you want to purchase or develop a new property or finance an existing one. There are two ways to do this: Either do it yourself or hire an expert.

DIYing your loan sourcing is cost-effective but involves a lot of groundwork. You have to research as many issuers as you possibly can, doing background checks and scouring through their site or visiting in person and talking to reps. You can start with a simple Google search or ask for recommendations from your close circles. Narrow to the best two or three, and then choose the best terms and conditions.

While this might save you lots of costs, you just can't escape certain fees, especially what are called loan points: a percentage of the total loan amount. Loan points are usually inversely proportional to the amount requested, so a $10 million loan will have a smaller loan point compared to a $1 million loan.

If you don't think you have the time or skills to source the best loan deal, you can enlist the help of mortgage brokers. These are commercial mortgage experts who can help you find the most suitable terms for any particular project. Besides their extensive experience with the mortgage capital market, mortgage brokers also have working relationships with many different lenders that you can leverage to get better terms and discounts.

Mortgage brokers usually charge about .5% to 2% of the loan amount – the higher the loan amount, the lower the percentage they charge.

MULTIFAMILY REFINANCING: PREPAYMENT OPTIONS AND PREPAYMENT PENALTIES

Now, the equity and the period it takes to generate it are the most important things an equity investor cares about, especially for those who repackage and resell loans in secondary markets. They want to be sure of how long their investment will be tied down as well as the yields that will come from it.

Their offer usually comes with the most optimal terms for them – pay the loan too early or too late, and they're in a less optimal position. So, they often impose fines for breaching the initial terms: prepayment fines for paying too early and default fines for payment delays.

Prepayment fines are usually more common than default fines because borrowers often prefer to lay down the debt burden sooner rather than later to free up positive cash flow on their property. If you pay earlier, you may be fined a percentage of the loan. This is to help the investor reinvest the capital in another venture to make up for the yields they'd have generated from the remaining period of your deal.

Prepayment fines aren't just some arbitrary figure named by the lender. A lot of calculation actually goes into them. The three most common prepayment formulas are the step-down calculation, yield maintenance, and the defeasance calculation.

With the step-down model, the penalty decreases the closer you approach the maturity date. So if you have a 10-year deal, you might have a 5% fee for paying in the first five years, 2% after seven years, and 1% after nine years.

The yield maintenance model is one of the most complex penalty models, but it's also very popular, used by the likes of Fannie Mae and Freddie Mac. It's complex, but you don't have to wring your head because there are many online calculators to help with the number crunching. You only have to enter the appropriate matrices in the right places, and the calculator takes care of the rest. So basically, yield maintenance is calculated by taking the yield that the loan would have generated in the remaining term and then calculating how much capital would be needed to generate that yield for the lender. Hence, the term "yield maintenance."

The defeasance model takes government bonds as the alternative investment vehicle that a lender will use to recover the remaining yields from a loan that has been prepaid. So what they'll do is calculate the amount needed to invest in government bonds in order to get the remaining yield. Lower bond interest rates mean a bigger defeasance penalty because the investor would need a bigger amount to generate similar yields. In most cases where the bond interest rate increases at the time of the repayment, the defeasance pay is usually smaller, and if the interest rate is higher compared to the loan rates, you'll probably not pay any fine because the investor can make more money from the government bond.

While many investors would prefer to collect prepayment fees, the good news is that it isn't always the case. Some multifamily loans don't come with any prepayment penalties. And those that do usually have a prepayment window where you won't face any charges. Charge-free prepayment windows usually range 9–18 months from maturity.

Also, keep in mind that prepayment windows have their direct opposite: lockout periods. Under no circumstance can you fully prepay your loans during a lockout period. Lockout periods are usually common with loans sold in secondary markets, where investors need to be guaranteed a certain yield over a period. Now, if you accept a very attractive refinancing or outright sale offer during the lockout period, you'll have to continue servicing the loan throughout the lockout period.

PRIVATE LENDING

Private finance companies are one of the single greatest assets that you can work with if you know how to use the money to make more money. However, conventional financing will usually get you better interest rates than private financiers. They will get you a better long-term holding strategy, but private financing is necessary if you are stuck in a pickle and want to get control and ownership of the property and have options. Private lenders don't want to foreclose on your property. They want you to succeed. They will guide you to succeed. They will tell you when you're making a bad financial decision, and they will not lend to you.

Additionally, new avenues in rental properties, like accessory dwelling units, are so far ahead of their time that conventional lenders often don't even know how to lend to them. For example, some appraisers for ADUs will just take the cost you have put in and a nominal amount above that and consider the increased value of your property. Meanwhile, another appraiser will say to base the price entirely on the square footage you've added to your property compared to the average cost per square foot in the area.

The moral of the story is that conventional finance companies, especially when dealing with recent legislative changes, don't know how to operate. You need private finance companies who can help you to figure out how to proactively solve a problem. If you pay a little premium for it, so be it. The lenders don't know how to protect their loans. The loan is predicated upon the collateral, which is the home with the increased value. That value is still subject to whoever is appraising that value, and their opinion can vary wildly.

Private financiers are less risk-averse than conventional lenders. They are a bit more willing to go deeper into a situation to figure out how to protect their money and extract the greatest outcome for the borrower. With adapt and reuse projects, it's hard to determine the value of a property previously operating as an office or retail space (with its own standards and metrics for traffic and income) that will now operate as a residential space. How much time and money will it take to change it from office space to residential space? Who is going to be lending that money for those changes? Who is going to be getting rid of the commercial footprint and putting in the plumbing for the kitchens and additional bathrooms? In an office building, you typically have one or two bathrooms for everyone in the office. Now, every unit needs its own bathroom.

There is a big disconnect between who has the money, how the money is going to be used, and how quickly the money is going to be returned. What will you do if you don't have a lender willing to do it? Even if you have enough of your own money to cover it, you will be 100% involved with little leverage, defeating one of the greatest strengths of rental property investing. Any time you convert another type of property to residential, money is going to have to be spent. Private lenders are there to bridge the gap when conventional lenders won't bear the risk.

Accredited high-net-worth groups or individuals usually fund private lenders. Their loans are often faster, as they do not require owner occupancy. They have more flexible terms, including a reduced down payment, short-term duration, interest-only payments, and longer amortization if needed. There are also a number of variables that can be customized with the lender to accommodate the needs of the loan. The right private lender may be more willing to work with you to achieve your needs by providing more flexibility, resulting in an easier and faster loan approval process with enhanced customer service. In a competitive market, an investor with the right relationship with their private lender can close more deals.

Since private lenders are smaller or operate independently, the decision-making process might be based more on intangibles rather than merely a review of income, assets, credit, and collateral. Private lending helps fill the void on deals that banks and other lending institutions will not or cannot do. Though usually more costly in origination fees and interest than conventional lenders, there may be savings in reduced or no prepay penalties or credit reporting that may limit your future options. At the very least, it is better to have options and not use them than no options at all.

Having a long-term goal in mind when you use a private money lender is key. In general, private money loans are not meant for long-term financing and don't offer terms longer than five years. Use the money for cash out, a bridge loan, a real estate improvement loan, or a property acquisition (purchase money) loan.

One of the most important things in a purchase transaction is speed. A direct lender with their own funds can fund in as little as two or three days when the valuation of the property is self-evident. Much of the time, an appraisal will be necessary as well, which could slow things down by seven to ten days. But typically, a private money loan is fast. The term for a private money loan is typically one to four years, so it's perfect for a fix-and-flip property. If you have a "keeper," you will need to refinance again in the short-term future with a conventional lender to keep your loan payments as low as possible.

Another example of what a private lender can do that a conventional lender can't is buying a property at a foreclosure auction. At a foreclosure auction, you are required to bring a cashier's check, cash, or cash equivalent (money orders) to purchase the property. Often, you can get a real bargain at a foreclosure auction sale by showing up in person to bid, but who has all the cash to pay? Here is where a private party lender comes in to help. A private lender can show up with you to produce loan proceeds at the time of purchase. It takes some coordination, but if you have a good relationship with your private party lender, they can make it happen.

Private money loans are almost always based on the property and much less on your financial condition. The downside is that the rate is going to be higher than what a bank can offer you. How much higher depends on the private money lender. If you look around, you may be able to find one that is just 1% or 2% over what the major banks charge.

Always have the private money lender give you a forward commitment in writing. This will make your offer the same as all cash to the seller, whereby your down payment will be accompanied by the forward commitment funds from the private money lender to escrow. Often, private money lenders close purchase money transactions in just a few days with only a Broker Opinion of Value substituting for a full appraisal, allowing you to make what is essentially an all-cash offer and close in seven working days. Your seller is going to be delighted, and you will beat out other offers contingent on bank financing.

Once you've decided a private lender is your best option, select one that aligns with your financial objectives. If the private lender's mindset, communication, guidance, and services are in sync with your objectives, you've got a winner. Follow through on your promises, communicate well, and make sure your private lender reciprocates. You are in a relationship and want your lender actively engaged and fully aware of the variables so they can aid you as much as possible, especially if you plan on doing more deals.

Private lenders will likely require much of the same paperwork as conventional lenders to assess your credit history, income, assets, and cash flow through recent bank statements. They will want to review average deposits in your account and the ebbs and flows of your monthly spending. More aggressive private lenders offering less down payment may seek your tax returns, profit-and-loss statements, or alternative proof of income.

Seller carryback is also a very useful option in many cases. If you can get your seller to carry your loan, this can be the best option of all. You get to avoid points, fees, and much of the paperwork. You're also likely to get a lower rate than a bank loan. Turn on your negotiating skills and sit down with your Realtor and seller to negotiate out favorable terms. Often, you can get an older seller to carry the loan by pointing out the advantages of the monthly payments coming in and having the money earn more interest than a savings account at the bank. Offering the seller a rate of 5% today is much more than any C/D. Often, a seller is just going to put the sales proceeds in their bank account to earn next to nothing. Suddenly, 5% sounds great. You can tell the seller that the loan is saleable at any time, and the longer it is "seasoned," the more valuable it becomes (much like how a savings bond getting closer to maturity date becomes more valuable).

If your seller needs all cash, you can point out they can sell the loan while in escrow and close with all cash. There are many private-party loan buyers out there. Many are the same private party lenders that we talked about earlier. Point out that the discount (if any) is tax-deductible against the gain the seller is taking on the property. Also, you can close your transaction with the seller lending the money. If the seller is exchanging out of the property to take advantage of a 1031 tax exchange or tax deferral transaction, the seller carryback loan MUST be sold in order to comply with IRS rules. A grace period of ten days is helpful to make the loan salable before a late fee of 5% or 6% is applied, as is a due-on-sale clause. All of this is negotiable, so think about what you want and practice what to say before approaching your Realtor or the seller.

The way I came to own my very first property, 433 Magnolia, was that the owner chose to let me take over payments for his loan. It was a small balance – about $183,000. I took it over in the form of subject-to financing. The loan stayed in his name with the lender even though I was making the payments. We did it this way because when I called the lender, they asked me to qualify with credit and show income. I would have also had to pay $5,000 to assume the loan officially in my name, which I didn't have at the time. A big concern with subject-to financing is that the loan documents make it possible to accelerate the loan and call it due at any time.

Unfortunately, what often happens with conventional multifamily lenders is that the deal you think you're going to get is ultimately not what they come through with. They might come back to you and tell you that the appraisal was too low and that the property's income is insufficient. In these cases, if you want to close on a deal, you might have to put an additional $100,000 or more down. I've missed out on many great buying opportunities and had to pivot in a new direction at the 11th hour when conventional lenders screwed me on appraisals, tax service, and everything they can change at the last minute. Everything can end up different than you've been led to believe.

CHAPTER 7
NEGOTIATING THE PURCHASE PROCESS

"The best negotiations occur when all parties
walk away feeling they've won."
—Tony Robbins

When it comes to negotiating with a seller, it's important to understand who they are and why they are selling their property. Some sellers may have owned the property for a long time and have refinanced it multiple times, while others may be newer owners who have made recent upgrades or faced administrative citations. The seller's permit history can also give insight into their property management experience.

Where the seller lives can be an important factor. Out-of-area sellers may not be as familiar with the micro-area conditions and may be less directly involved in managing the property. They may also have less personal attachment to the property, making it easier to negotiate.

Understanding the seller's profession and financial situation can also help negotiate a deal. For example, some medical professionals such as doctors and dentists may be high-income earners looking for tax write-offs and may be more hands-off with the property.

Overall, taking the time to build rapport and understand the seller's motivations can lead to a mutually beneficial outcome in negotiations. It's important to communicate effectively and operate with an attitude of gratitude and respect to avoid leaving a negative stigma and reputation in the industry.

Most people don't get into the position of selling their property just because they want to sell. It often comes down to one of the three unfortunate Ds: death, divorce, or destitution. Maybe someone received a property through inheritance after the death of a family member and has no interest in managing it. Estate sales are common in these situations. Or maybe as someone gets older and their health fails, they'd rather free up their time and use the money for something else than hold onto an old property. During or after a divorce, the owner of a property can become entangled in lawsuits and disagreements that prevent them from holding onto it. Destitution and the pressing need for money can come from many sources, including bankruptcy and foreclosure. Buildings get condemned all the time due to new regulations or deteriorating conditions. Or maybe someone is just ready to move to a far-off location or retire from the business and rest on their laurels. In fact, the average lifespan of a homeowner is only about seven years. For multi-family properties, there may be a longer holding period where people just buy it and hold onto it for 20, 30, 40, or 50 years.

By taking the time to build rapport and real relationships with sellers instead of just faxing in offers, you will much better understand their motivations and perspective. If the seller is willing to take the time to sit down with you, you can learn how best to address their needs and the reasons they are selling in the first place. Do they want to go into a triple-net lease in Wisconsin? Do they have family there? Do they want to cash out and leave the money for their children because they are afraid of dying? If you know their wants and concerns, including where they want to be and why they're doing what they're doing, you can write your offer in a way that benefits them and you. It's not a completely zero-sum game. It's about communication and putting in the work to be able to understand the seller's and the owner's objectives.

In fact, as you ask more questions, your own objectives may change. As you're starting to get input and understand the psyche of someone in the position you're going to be in once you become an owner, you can better hone your own reality as a seller someday.

Understanding the seller's perspective even has a major effect on negotiating the price and terms of the property you are interested in. Through proper empathetic negotiation, you can find a mutually beneficial outcome. The last thing you want to do is leave behind a negative stigma that may cause a bad reputation to follow you around. In an industry as big as real estate, it can still feel quite small. You always want to operate with an attitude of gratitude and respect, a clarity of conduct.

ESSENTIAL INFORMATION FOR THE NEGOTIATING PROCESS

There are many questions you'll ideally want to ask the seller when you start to go through with the purchase process of their property. You should be putting in enough sweat equity by knocking on doors with "For Rent" signs, speaking to owners and going into homes, meeting spouses and looking at photos of the kids, and hearing about their pains and their problems, all in service of getting to understand them a little bit more. All of this is an important part of communication and rapport building.

You can start with something as simple as writing down notes on a napkin over lunch with the seller. Does the seller have a price in mind? What is the reason they're selling? What would make them interested if they're not currently interested in selling? How much would you like to offer them and why?

The more you parse out before just writing an offer and the more questions you ask, the greater you can calibrate your offer to the seller's needs (as long as they remain in line with your needs). If they are not in line with your own needs, you can give counter-proposals based on data sets you provide that help support an argument you make. Before even writing up an offer, you have to have a better understanding of the property's neighborhood. You should have planned out what value you can add to the property.

You'll need to have enough money for a 3% initial deposit. The deposits can go up to $100,000 if it's a larger multifamily deal. You can contact your local escrow if you do not have a real estate agent. Tell them you're looking at buying some properties and that you're not working with any real estate agents. You want to find your own deals. Do they have a template you can use to write up offers with potential buyers, and are they comfortable with you sending the escrow to them to be that neutral third-party intermediary for the purchase?

One of the best things escrow companies do is customer service, including handling details in the paperwork. So, having a great escrow officer on your side is a huge asset and can be an important part of the process. An escrow officer will be great if you're young, motivated, and willing to do the work.

Escrow officers are experts in the field of real estate transactions and can provide valuable guidance throughout the process. They can help you navigate the complexities of the process, including preparing and reviewing documents, managing timelines, and communicating with all parties involved. Working closely with your escrow officer can help streamline the process and make it more efficient. They can help identify potential roadblocks or issues early on, allowing you to address them before they become major problems.

Escrow officers act as a central point of communication for all parties involved in the transaction. By building a strong relationship with your escrow officer, you can ensure that you are kept informed and up-to-date on the status of the transaction. If unexpected issues arise during the transaction, your escrow officer can help you find solutions.

Search on the internet for purchase agreements or contracts for your state. If you still don't have a real estate agent, you'll want to figure out how to write an offer. Go on training sites like Udemy or visit relevant Facebook groups to better understand what a proper offer looks like. What's included in an offer? What's excluded? Why are offers written the way they are?

After all that work, it may turn out that the seller wants to use a real estate agent. Real estate agents, as I said before, do a great job, but they do have to add value. They typically do this by representing the seller and increasing the purchase price. They must increase the price by an amount greater than their commission to justify their involvement.

I make it a habit to write offers well below a property's asking price, knowing full well that I'm almost certainly not going to make a deal. I do it to be able to get a sense of what the state of the economy is. If the stock or cryptocurrency market crashes, it might make people more desperate for quick cash. They might be willing to sell for less. If I'm in a strong cash position when this happens, my offers might only be 60% to 70% of what they should be. The seller might ignore my lowball offers at first. But at some point, they're going to start countering. When nobody else is at the table, I get to dictate the terms of the deal.

Making frequent offers is part of being in the game. It helps you stay sharp. It forces you to always be out there fighting and getting information, which gives you a powerful competitive advantage in real estate.

Eventually, you start looking for certain indicators that help you decide which properties to make offers on. For example, I always move quickly on listings with agents from outside the local area. Odds are good that they won't know what they're doing. They typically don't know the local market and the value of the property they're representing. If you find a property for sale with an out-of-area agent, you can probably end up getting a better deal than you normally would.

SETTING PRICE AND TERMS

Everything in this world that people decide is negotiable, even petty things you would probably never think to put up a fuss over. The world looks very different when you apply this mentality to everything. You stop accepting that things are how they are at face value. Instead, you imagine all the other ways it's within your control to negotiate them to be.

In a certain sense, every human interaction is a negotiation. When you want someone to give you something or do something for you, you must somehow create the conditions that will make them inclined to give you what you want. When you see items sold in mass quantities at fixed prices, you naturally assume that's just how things should be. But somewhere in the chain of command, there is a person who controls that price and has the discretion to change it under the right conditions. Every organization in the world has people at or near the top making similar decisions about how every facet of it is run.

Of course, that's not to say that it's in your best interest to go out of your way to argue over every little thing in life. Just because everything *can* be negotiated doesn't mean it *should* be. In most cases, it probably wouldn't be worth the time and other resources you'd have to invest into the process for a relatively small outcome in your favor. Other times, you might hurt yourself in the long term by benefiting in the short term, such as if the person you are negotiating with walks away with a lower opinion of you and feels less inclined to want to work with you again.

Things that seem like incompatible goals between negotiating parties are often not actually incompatible. It might require a lot of creative, out-of-the-box thinking to figure out how to arrange things so that everyone gets what they most want.

The way a negotiation works out is highly subject to how much information each party has about the other, including what they want and what they are willing to give up to get it. Information is power. The more of it you have, the better your bargaining position will be. Generally, the inverse is also true; you don't want the other party to have too much information about you because it gives them potentially greater leverage over you. But this isn't strictly the case in all situations. Sometimes, by sharing more information than you have to, it's easier to build trust and rapport, which leads to faster and better resolutions.

This is often the case in my negotiations when I am trying to sell one of my properties. I know that if I go out of my way to tell the prospective buyer about potential problems they may face with the building down the road that they don't already know about, their respect for me goes up tremendously. They are more willing to take me at my word and treat me fairly. This is a core component of being a likable and relatable person, which can greatly benefit negotiations.

Some of the most important information you can know to make a negotiation more likely to work out in your favor is the timeline limitations of the other party compared to your own. If you have more time on your hands than the other party, you have the advantage. Typically, if you go to a car lot with the intent of making a purchase, you'll find the process takes many more hours than you anticipated. But if you go on a Friday night near their closing time at the end of the month, you'll find that they are much more likely to want to speed up the process and close a deal as quickly as possible. They don't want to stay extra hours after work for a sale that might not happen, and salespeople have an incentive to close as many deals as possible by the end of any given calendar month.

As I've gotten older, I've been able to stash away millions of dollars for putting into properties that are below market value. I want underutilized real estate investments that haven't reached their full potential value. They're perfect for investors who are looking to make money by increasing value. But to make this work, I have to know how to negotiate. If you don't know how to negotiate, you're going to hit a wall and not know how to get around it.

EMPATHY AND MANIPULATION

The first principle to understand about negotiation is seeing things from the other party's perspective. If you've got the wherewithal and the goal to achieve something, and you understand the limiting factors of the other party, you can use that to gain leverage over them. If I know the seller has to sell by a certain date (or incur hundreds of thousands of dollars in tax liability), and if there are no other buyers, I know that I can delay my decision-making as part of the negotiation. I know that I'm in control of the timeline of the sale. As it gets closer to the due date, there's a greater time sensitivity, which will allow me to extract greater savings on the price of the property. If you know the other person's timeline and limitations, you can use that to your advantage in a zero-sum exchange.

I don't want you to take that advice the wrong way. I don't mean to be predatory and seek to take advantage of sellers in bad positions and cause them to lose. Empathy is also a very important aspect of buyer/seller relationships. But, often, in high-value situations, empathy quickly becomes less important to helping you get the most of what you want out of the deal. I try as often as possible to look for win-win proposals, but that is moderately disingenuous because sometimes you really do have to go for the jugular to make a deal equitable at all for you and make the exchange happen. If you don't know how to do it and other people are willing to do it to you, you will be ill-equipped to be able to survive in a world of predators. You will be at a tactical disadvantage.

There have been many times when I would go into a car dealership and try to negotiate with predators to my great disadvantage. They sit you down and ask you what car you like. They get you to go through all these cars and look at models you don't even like. As soon as you say, "Oh, I like that car." They pressure you into taking it for a test drive. Of course, they need to take your driver's license for that to happen. So now they're holding onto your license. You drive the car, and then they make you wait while you mull over whether you want to buy it. They'll offer you a glass of water. They know about the law of reciprocity: that people naturally want to give something back any time somebody's given something.

At that point, you're likely to be thinking, "Okay, well, I can't very well leave now. They've given me a test drive. I've taken up their time, and I'm drinking a glass of their water." Because they've made you wait so long, you've invested 30 minutes to an hour into this process, which makes you naturally reluctant to just walk away and waste all that time. But the truth is that they already have everything they need. They just make you keep waiting to put you at a psychological disadvantage in the negotiation.

Through prolonged negotiation, their goal is to get you into a state of mind where you are saying to yourself, "Well, damn, I've already been here for two or three hours. I didn't really like the car coming in, but the opportunity cost of the time wasted is too important to me. I don't want it to have been for nothing, so maybe I will buy this car." The point is that in any form of negotiation, one of the best tricks is taking control of your opponent's time and using it against them.

Then there's the factor of competition. If you're a seller, you can take a lot of the pressure off yourself and expand your timeline by seeking out as many buyers and offers as possible. Once you get together however many buyers you're able to source, you can write up multi-family counters to each of them, letting them know that they need to give better prices because there are so many offers for your property. If the negotiations go on long enough, the remaining buyers adopt the emotional temperament of someone who's invested so much of themselves into the process that they're highly incentivized to go through with a purchase, even at a price much higher than they initially thought they'd be willing to pay.

No matter which side of the exchange you are on, much of the negotiation process depends on how much wherewithal you have to try to make the deal work in your favor. If a seller doesn't have any other buyers, they may be willing to just keep going down that rabbit hole with you as their only precious buyer. Of course, they may also kick you to the curb. It's the nature of all business. Everyone is trying to mitigate their risk and get the best deal they can in every situation.

You can always sharpen your negotiating chops by writing more and more offers. The more offers that you write, the more responses you will get. Some of those counters will be far lower than you thought the seller would offer.

A friend of mine who was new to rental properties fell into the amateurish habit of just automatically countering each asking price with some arbitrary amount less. If a property was $169,000, he'd simply offer $159,000 and be done with it, assuming he'd be getting a good deal by going under the asking price. I'd encourage him to take a little more risk with his offers. I told him to try countering at $99,000 instead. He was worried about offending the seller by going so low. To my friend's surprise, the sellers countered at $139,000—a full $10,000 less than he said he would pay. But I told my friend not to give in yet. He countered at $109,000, which was promptly countered with $119,000.

The moral of the story is to learn how to hunt. Learn how to negotiate and know that each seller and each buyer have their own independent mechanisms for why they're selling, what price point they're selling at, and what terms they're selling at.

Negotiating is a large part of real estate, and many investors and owners in this space overlook its importance. The buyer and seller are going to agree on a price at some point, but why not spend a few more minutes on due diligence when it could easily amount to a large difference in the price? If you strengthen your communication skills, you'll be able to interact better. You'll be able to save more money, make more money, get more shit done, and spend your time on what it is better suited for.

KEY TAKEAWAYS FOR NEGOTIATING THE BEST DEAL

1. Do thorough research and understand the values of the property or assets being negotiated.
2. Understand the perspective and needs of the other party in order to find mutually beneficial solutions.
3. Communicate openly and honestly and listen actively to the other party.
4. Focus on the underlying interests driving each party's position rather than positions themselves.
5. Look for common ground and areas of agreement to build on.
6. Be flexible and open to compromise while also having clear boundaries and deal-breakers.
7. Use objective criteria to guide decision-making and avoid misunderstandings.
8. Consider seeking the help of a mediator or arbitrator if negotiations become stuck.

CHAPTER 8

MAXIMIZING VALUE WITH AMENITIES AND UPGRADES

"The bitterness of poor quality remains long after the sweetness of low price is forgotten."
—Benjamin Franklin

You finally own it. Now what?

The list of possible improvements, renovations, or amenities to add to a property is endless. So, how do you strategically choose which ones to focus on? How do you know which changes will actually affect your bottom line and improve the perception of the quality of your property from your tenants' perspective? Even if they are in the same area and of roughly the same size, why can some units command much higher rents and maintain a much lower vacancy rate? Why should investors be willing to pay more for some properties and expect greater income and appreciation over time than other properties?

In other words: How do you get the most bang for your buck?

When I started, I would just slap some paint on the walls, scrape the popcorn ceilings, and put in linoleum or vinyl flooring. Maybe I'd also change the toilet and shower head if they were old for new low-flow models. However, as I've gotten more experience in this business, I've come to realize that people are willing to pay more and it will be easier to find tenants if I do more than the bare minimum to improve my units. The more improvement you put into your property and the greater pride of ownership you take, the greater competitive advantage you will have over other properties.

"Pride of ownership" is a concept attributed to owners who take great care of their properties because they see it as an extension of who they are. These are the people providing valuable places to live. Any owner could rent out an apartment in poor condition to someone desperate enough to take it, but would they feel good about their role in that relationship?

Slum lords have very low pride in ownership. They focus almost exclusively on getting the highest cash flow for the lowest amount of work, investment, and loss of time. They don't put money back into their properties and most likely don't concern themselves with improving the quality of life for their residents.

Ironically, these owners are leaving money on the table if they don't consider how putting money back into their properties will enable them to make more in the long run. Well-kept rental properties rent faster, at higher rates. They stay occupied longer with a lower rate of tenant turnover. Furthermore, by taking care of your investment, you will raise the standard for other properties in your area, which raises the market value and rental rate of your own property. It's the start of a positive feedback loop that benefits you and everyone around you. If you are going to get involved in the rental property game, I advocate playing it as well as you possibly can, and that means having high pride of ownership for what you own.

There are many common renovations to multifamily units, such as new hardware like countertops and cabinets, new furniture like couches and beds, new appliances, or even an entirely new floor if needed. Each improves the quality of life for tenants, justifying a higher monthly rental rate and giving them all the more reason to stay with you for the long term. However, you need to be especially aware of the investment you will have to make to improve every unit in your building. You can easily burn a hole in your budget trying to make every unit as nice as it can be with the expectation that raised rents will more than make up for your expenses. But that depends on the area you've chosen to invest in and what local tenants can reasonably afford and would be willing to pay for. If you raise your rents high enough, you'll eventually price yourself out of the market.

Proximity to employment and universally desired social amenities is always a big occupancy driver. With more people working online, convenient access to restaurants, coffee shops, bookstores, bars, or other commonly enjoyed forums shapes one's living situation more than almost any other single factor. The more convenient the location of the property, the higher rent the owner can charge because there will be greater demand from tenants.

You'll also tend to find higher rents on units with great views. Different tenants will be more inclined toward different kinds of views (cityscape, the ocean, trees, etc.). The main thing is having something nicer than a brick wall or dark alley to look out your windows at. But even if that's all you have to work with, there are always creative ways that you can increase the value of an otherwise undesirable view. Paint a mural on a drab wall. Add plants and benches in an alley to make it feel more like a cozy backyard. You can even try to turn it into a tourist attraction.

However, generating more income through raised rents isn't the only reason to upgrade your units. Certain types of hardware improvements actually save you money in maintenance and repair because they are less likely to incur damage or are just cheaper to fix. Everything breaks over time, but sometimes, a larger upfront expense in more durable countertops or floors means saving yourself replacement costs over the long term. You could easily add several years of life to many aspects of each unit.

The biggest problem as a rental property investor is letting properties sit vacant for extended periods of time because you haven't figured out how to improve them, price them, and present them to the market. A lot of new owners get paralyzed by all the options. The confusion prevents them from taking any action at all. They don't want to have to deal with talking to painters, getting bids, not liking any of the options, and then starting the process all over again. Meanwhile, the units are sitting empty the whole time and not producing income. To really make this business work, you've got to be prepared. You've got to get your act together and act efficiently to minimize vacancy time.

That's the main reason owners typically consider managing property to be an onerous experience and end up hiring property management companies. Property management companies have experienced maintenance staff. They have their plans in line. They have everything streamlined down to just a few effective choices. Increase the electric outlets. Put in a nice tile backsplash in the kitchen. Add new cabinets, new furnishings, finishings, and lighting.

If your goal is to buy a polished pig already in pristine condition and for which there is little you can do to add value, that's your discretion. With any property, whether it's an Ugly Betty or the purest, most awesome building out there, you're going to have income. Further still, you're probably going to have more income with a nicer property. However, as you spend more money on your property, you're going to be able to depreciate more and/or have more expenses, and those expenses go against your taxes. You get write-offs from all of those expenses and improvements.

The better the property appears, the more of a competitive advantage you have over less nice properties. Being a 10-out-of-10 quality building when most others are 5s, 6s, or 7s makes yours stand out and justifies a higher rental rate. As well, your equity is most likely going to grow. Increasing the rent increases the income, and rental property values are partially based on their income.

Over the past 25 years, I've grown greatly in my experience in construction, but I was horrible when I started. To this day, I still have trouble hanging blinds. But I've known from the beginning of my foray into rental properties that I have the brains and the intuition to find people who know what they are doing better than I do. I know to get the best people to work with their best strengths so that I can work with mine. My strength is that I ask questions. I learn. I collect things, information, and ideas. I use that to my advantage to make strategic decisions to maximize an outcome. And I communicate my vision to others.

Coming up, I'll give you a few examples from my own experience of how making the right improvements can improve your tenants' quality of life, your monthly rental income, and, ultimately, how much you can sell a property for when you're done with it.

THE COMMON PITFALLS OF FAILING TO MAXIMIZE RENTS

Maximizing rents means charging the highest amount the market will bear for each unit and operating at full capacity. It means getting the most recurring income you can from your asset. If you know that a unit at your property could be rented for $2,000 per month, but the current resident is paying only $1,800, you are missing out on 10% of the maximum rent. This is common with tenants who sign long-term leases and lock in a low rate at a time when the market is rapidly getting more expensive. They keep paying the low rate until their lease expires and can be renewed at the increased market rate.

Locking in leases at below-market rates like this can be a great strategy for new owners trying to fill a mostly empty property as quickly as possible. After all, finding enough tenants to fill every unit at the market rate might take a long time. That would mean no rent from those vacant units during those months. Another common marketing tactic is offering a month or two rent-free concession when a new tenant signs a lease for a year or more. You'll be losing the income from the free months you offer, but it goes a long way toward filling vacant units quickly and keeping them occupied longer.

Remember that merely keeping your units full is not enough to indicate that you are doing the best you could be doing as a rental property owner. If you have 0% vacancy on a 100-unit property but only charge half the market rate, you might as well have 50% vacancy at the full market rate. Actually, that would be better because it would be easier to manage, and you would have fewer operating expenses. One benefit of a property management company is that they are in a position to help you determine what the market rates actually are and how much to charge for rent.

When one of my long-time-occupied one-bedroom units finally became vacant, I took the opportunity to redesign it. We got in there and put in brand-new hexagonal tiles and amazing quartz countertops. We made the hardwood floor look classy. Before, the unit had been rented for $1,200, the market rate. My partner and I went back and forth many times about how much higher the new rent rate should be, considering our improvements. Between the two of us, we had about 50 years of experience in rental units. We agreed it was time to go above the market rate of $1,200 because the unit was now much nicer than the market. Still, we didn't want to risk having it sit vacant while we looked for an appropriate renter who could afford it. We opted to pay for some sponsored advertising to get it in front of the right people, including some premium-quality photos to show off its upgraded value.

Even though we were a bit apprehensive about raising the price so much, we were pleasantly surprised to find three applicants on the very first day. From that, we learned that if we have a superior product, there's a demand for it. Maybe it won't be an overwhelming demand, but those who know the neighborhood and the product will be willing to pay the premium. It's always worth testing to see if you can go higher. After all, you can always lower the rent if it sits vacant for too long. It's much harder to raise the rent once you've offered it for a lower price.

Also, you have to consider how your ability to maximize your rental income will affect the property's sale price when it comes time to exit. Buyers will use your property's total monthly rent and the local gross rent multiplier (GRM) to determine how much they should pay for your property. This is essentially how many years of rent at full occupancy you'd have to collect before you make back the money you spent purchasing the property. Bear in mind that this doesn't take into account other expenses like utilities, maintenance, insurance, and taxes. It's just the gross rent amount in total. All other things being equal, the less time you have to wait for the building to pay for itself (the lower the GRM), the better. GRM can be calculated with either monthly or annual rental income, though annual tends to be more useful, as most properties take several years at the very least to pay for themselves.

GRM is most useful as a valuation tool when it's easy to predict what your other expenses will be over the period you will be renting it out, though this is impossible to predict with certainty. A few hundred dollars in lost rent per unit every month can turn into tens of thousands of dollars sitting on the table when selling. It's possible to try to argue what the pro forma rents of the units *should be* when setting a selling price, but lenders are much more likely to use the actual rates they are being rented at. So buyers are left with the burden of coming up with the extra cash on their own based on speculation about how much they could rent the units for.

Other contract details you can include to protect yourself and maximize income:

- Include a lease termination fee in the rental agreement to cover the costs of finding a new tenant if the current tenant decides to break the lease.
- Charge a holding fee to secure a unit for a prospective tenant while the landlord conducts a background check.
- Collect application fees from prospective tenants to cover the cost of background checks.
- Implement extra occupant fees for any additional adults who move into the rental unit after the lease has been signed. Be sure to conduct a background check and update the lease for the new occupant.
- Implement a fee for late rent payments.
- Charge a cleaning fee at the end of a tenancy to cover the cost of deep cleaning the unit.
- Increase rent on a regular basis, such as annually or every few years, to keep up with inflation or market demand.
- Consider renting out any unused space, such as a basement or garage, for an additional fee.
- Offer furnished units for a higher rent.
- Implement fees for any amenities or services provided to tenants, such as a gym or pool.
- Offer a lease renewal bonus or discount to encourage tenants to sign a new lease.
- Implement a fee for early termination of a lease.

CHECKING OUT THE COMPETITION

Start to keep your eyes open for rental signs. Read their listed prices and call to compare those properties to others in a similar price range. Does the property offer parking? How much do they charge for it? How big is the security deposit? Are utilities included? Is there a washer and dryer?

Know what is going on in your neighborhood. I like to walk around in the sunshine and see the rental signs, the quality of the property, and how good the general upkeep is. I look at the cars in the neighborhood, how they're kept and where they're parked, and if the registration is current, just to get an indication of what type of tenant base will be around.

I like to know the square footage, whether it's a studio, a single, a one-bedroom, a junior one-bedroom, a two-bedroom, or something else. Are the two-bedrooms on title as two-bedrooms? Or were they converted into multiple bedrooms from just one? Do they have hardwood flooring? Do they have tile floors in the kitchen and bathroom? Do they have upgraded countertops? Is it an energy-efficient property? Do they offer other amenities like free Wi-Fi, or is there solar on the property where the tenants don't have to pay for their own electricity?

What exactly makes a particular neighborhood upscale and more expensive to rent in? It could be closer to the beach or public transit. It could be closer to a bar. It could be closer to some other amenity that improves the quality of life. I like to buy properties that are near schools because schools denote children, children denote parents, and parents with children denote stability. They don't want to be moving frequently. If you find properties that have "for rent" signs constantly popping up, there's a reason people are moving.

You can also peruse apps or websites that deal in real estate. Apartments.com, Redfin, Zillow, and others are all great options. Limit your search to just your neighborhood so that you won't waste a lot of time in areas you don't understand. Try to understand the home values around you. Go to the open houses. Keep your eyes open for "for rent" and "for sale" signs. Pay particular attention to the sloppy and handwritten ones, as that usually indicates an independent operator instead of a professional management company. These properties usually have more potential to add value to and improve their processes, thereby increasing the rent.

Now ask yourself: Why is one studio apartment renting for $1,200 a month and another of similar size for $1,500? It probably isn't about the location since they are both in your neighborhood. Is it the condition? Is it the amenities? Does one of them have a spectacular view that the other does not? Does one have a move-in special with a lower security deposit?

Why is this exercise so important? Because as you get to know your market better, you will start to understand why some properties rent successfully at higher rates than others. You might then start to identify certain properties that experience tells you *should* be renting for more than they currently are. Many buildings are underperforming assets that could pull in much more income with a little effort and repositioning. If all four units in a building are renting at $1,200 a month and you can get them each up to $1,500, you will have successfully added $14,400 a year in value to it.

As you walk through the various properties, keep your eyes open for what aspects of their functionality and appearance stand out to you as dated or sub-optimal compared to modern standards. It could be the style of the ceilings or lighting. It could be ratty old shower curtains instead of a modern glass shower enclosure. Does a property have old pink floor tiles from the 1950s when that color was popular?

In all of these cases, you can begin to make the assessment that tenants might be willing to pay more for a place to live that looks contemporary and has more of the creature comforts that have become standard. It's not too hard to do some online research or go down to your local Home Depot and figure out the most popular modern aesthetic choices, even if you don't have direct experience in this area.

COMMON AMENITIES

What about providing the type of lifestyle amenities or utilities you can pre-dict that tenants will be going out of their way to acquire in their own units? If it's cheaper and more convenient for you to outfit all units in your property with wifi, it could create an incentive for tenants to choose to rent from you rather than to pick a place that requires them to set it up and maintain it them-selves. The same applies to washers and dryers, air conditioning units, and other ubiquitous appliances that almost everyone uses.

Adequate parking space is a frequently overlooked aspect of rental build-ings, especially in larger cities with denser populations. It's obvious that peo-ple who own cars would prefer to live somewhere they know they will always be able to reliably park their cars when they return home each day. This one addition alone can justify a significant increase in rental price.

One property had a 15-space parking lot that wasn't charging a fee for parking. All that needed to be done was install a gate with clickers and a ring camera and hand them out to the residents. Some (but not all) of the residents were even thankful not to have to fight or worry about which parking space they would get, if any. Then, if they wanted to be able to park there, they could pay a service charge of $100 per month. So, that quickly turned into $1,500 times 12 months ($18,000) additional cash flow for each year. Using a typical gross rate multiplier for the neighborhood, we ended up with $18,000 multiplied by 13 for a total increase in value of $234,000. From that added $234,000 in value, I could refinance the property, lock in a low, long-term rate, get my equity out, and leave it with cash flowing in a very low equity position. I was making more money with less of my own being tied up in it.

Do you allow pets in your units? If not, why not? You may have reasonable concerns about cats or dogs causing property damage or leaving hair and waste around the unit, but these concerns are largely exaggerated. Most pets don't cause more mess or damage than typical children. If they do end up scratching up the drywall or furniture, you can always take an additional security deposit to cover this possibility. Making your property pet-friendly greatly increases the likelihood that pet lovers will work extra hard to stay in one of your units long-term. It's an extremely easy way to stand out and be more desirable than similar properties that don't allow for the possibility of furry companions.

OPTIMIZING LIVING SPACE

Those are many other creative ways to add value. The average one-bedroom unit in Long Beach is between 400 and 500 square feet. If I've got a building full of one-bedrooms that are well over the average size at 800 square feet, how can I optimize the value for my tenants, thus justifying the highest possible rent? The average monthly rate for a one-bedroom in the area is $1,500. It will be hard for me to squeeze out $1,800 from a one-bedroom, even if it's larger than most because tenants won't necessarily care.

By adding a wall and a closet to each unit, I can convert them all into two-bedroom units, thus adding substantial value. The market rate for a two-bedroom in the area is about $2,300. I'm effectively getting $500 per month more than I would have if I had left them as one-bedroom units, and my tenants still feel like they are getting a good deal. You can apply the same logic by converting two-bedrooms into three-bedrooms and so on if the space allows for it.

In how many ways can you open up unused space in your units to make the living area larger? Can you convert a one-bedroom unit into a two-bedroom unit by converting an existing room into a sleeping space? The extra bedroom might be worth substantially more to renters than a room that would otherwise seldom be used, such as a formal dining room. In times when people are spending more and more time at home, making the most out of every square inch is important to your tenants' quality of life. The happier your tenants are and the more your property offers that other properties do not, the more demand there will be for your units. The more demand, the higher the rental price you can justify, and the less likely tenants are to move out soon, which means you'll save on lost revenue from non-occupancy and maintenance costs.

Shared outdoor living areas should be given almost as much credence as private indoor ones. By taking the time and effort to make common areas into enclosed patios or similarly nice spaces for tenants to hang out, you provide your renters with a feeling of luxury and comfort. Recreational outdoor space is something normally reserved for expensive private residences.

CASE STUDY: 433 MAGNOLIA

433 Magnolia was an eight-unit, two-story property built in the 1920s that I bought under the conditions of a "subject-to" deal. This means the investor receives the title, but the loan remains with the seller. It often happens when someone is behind on their payments. I bring their payments current, and I improve their credit. I become an all-inclusive trustee, which means I send them the payment for the mortgage, and they make the payments. However, sometimes, the seller absconds with the mortgage money instead of making their payment. I usually don't find out about this until a couple of months later, when the lender sends over a notice of default on the property.

When I took this property over, six of the eight units were vacant due to severe water and electrical damage. One of the two occupied units belonged to the onsite manager. She was seven months pregnant and eager to leave and go back to her home country. The result is that the owner was in a position where they dearly did not want to deal with the property any longer.

The first thing I did when I bought the place was move in a plumber and an electrician to one of the vacant units. They both needed a place to live, so I allowed them to work off their rent by working on the various problems around the building. Once the remaining units had the water and electricity in working order, I rented them out at a below-market rate. They were livable but still in substandard condition, justifying a rent discount for people looking to save some money. The nice thing about this setup was that my tenants didn't mind the noise the contractors made at night because they were getting such a great deal on the rent.

This was around the year 2000. I was still in college at this time, so I didn't have a lot of time to deal with managing the property. I ended up hiring a property management company, but ultimately, I had to fire them because they had tons of hidden fees for vendors like exterminators, making dealing with them too expensive.

I went to an MLS to find the agent with the most sales and list them with them. That seems like pretty solid reasoning. If they have the most sales, they must be the best. Right? But I saw the error in my thinking when I received three offers on the first day of its listing. It hit me then that my agent had listed it too cheap to secure a quick sale without considering that I would be willing to wait longer to get more for it.

One of those offers was from a professor at UCLA named Tom Lewis, who happened to be the father of Jeff Lewis, a world-renowned home renovator and flipper on a nationally syndicated TV show called Flipping Out. We ended up partnering up on the property, and I agreed to pay for the fix-up costs. At the time, the property was listed for $425,000, and I had paid only $183,000 for it. Our goal was to figure out how to put the minimum amount of improvements into it to add the most market value. We ultimately repositioned its price to $699,000, which was settled with a loan of $575,000, a Seller 2nd of $41,000, and a Seller 3rd of $50,000. After the deal, I ended up relinquishing the 3rd TD (Trust Deed) to Tom Lewis and kept the $575,000 proceeds to 1031 exchange into 617 West 7th and 433 West 4th Street.

As my real estate mentor, Tom showed me how to increase the property's value by approximately $300,000. I was able to carry that understanding forward with all my other properties. I messed up many times but did what truly mattered correctly: tying up the deal, not having paralysis by analysis, and figuring out on the fly how to extract the highest value.

CASE STUDY: 617 WEST 7TH STREET

617 West 7th Street was an 18-unit apartment building comprised of five buildings, each with its own underground garage. One of the buildings faced a busy street, on the other side of which sat an elementary school. It had separate metered gas and electric, so the tenants paid their own utilities.

With such a large building with so many units that needed similar renovations in each one, I was able to take advantage of a significant economy of scale advantage. It was easy to convince the carpet company to give me a nice discount on the cost of re-carpeting all 18 units compared to if I had to do it one unit at a time due to the greater volume.

This building had popcorn ceilings, which sometimes have a carcinogenic substance in them. As such, the typical thing to do is hire a company specializing in changing it to something more modern. I was too cheap to deal with that at the time, so I learned how to spackle a ceiling with a friend over a single night with the help of a bottle of tequila. You can imagine that we both had the sorest shoulders of our lives the next morning. That experience taught me the true value of being able to outsource the labor to someone who knows what they are doing and will save me the trouble of doing it myself, even if it costs me a bit more.

When we were done with the refurbishments, we raised the rent a bit to what we considered appropriate. However, even though we were still under the market rate, many of our tenants were not happy with the increase. So, I tried to come up with a solution that would make them happy and save me the trouble of having to find new tenants. I devised a program where they chose between different upgrades to their apartments. Their options included amenities like a ceiling fan or a glass shower enclosure in lieu of a curtain or an air conditioning unit. That upgrade benefited me because it increased the value of the property and benefited the occupants because it made them more comfortable at home and more tolerable of the rent prices.

If they had children, for example, they often got tired of the kids splashing everywhere in the bathtub all over the floor. Those are the ones who were more likely to choose the glass shower enclosure. In the case of tenants who were a little on the older side, they tended to be more prone to wanting a cooler environment at home. So, they chose the air conditioning. But they chose the ceiling fan if they didn't want to get stuck having to pay the electric bill (because they were responsible for their own utilities). In any case, some people did move out, but we were usually able to fill those empty units for 10% to 40% more than previously.

CASE STUDY: 433 WEST 4TH STREET

Next, I partnered up with my friend Brian again to buy 433 West 4th Street, a 12-unit apartment building. The seller of the property at the time was Robert Abassi, who owned RTI Properties. He agreed to sell the property to me for $665,000. We ended up putting 25% down at that price.

We did a number of remodels inside and got beat up in expenses throughout. We weren't experienced enough then to know the true cost of drywall, painting, or even electrical. We were very fortunate in this case not to have to deal with anyone from the Air Quality Management District (AQMD). They are the people who get called about asbestos, lead, or other harmful materials in the air of older buildings that were made before we knew these things were dangerous. A single violation can carry a $25,000 fee, and then I would have to go take classes and get my hands slapped.

Fortunately, one of my tenants, who happened to be a handyman, wanted some repairs done to his unit, and he offered to do them himself. He eventually became my maintenance supervisor. Working together, we learned many lessons about controlling costs, ensuring maintenance work is done correctly, and ensuring that estimates are accurate and in writing.

A number of the units had one large bedroom with a den, which is common with a lot of 1920s construction. We converted some of the living space into a second bedroom and increased the rent from $700 to $1,300 per month. Any time you can increase the monthly income on a property like this, you increase the property's value, too. If you can reduce the expenses, you also increase the property's value. Ultimately, after 11 months of owning the property and repositioning four of the units, we put it on the market for $1,350,000. We got an offer, and it was sold at $1,250,000.

CHAPTER 9

MANAGING THE PROPERTY

"It's far better to buy a wonderful company at a fair price than a fair company at a wonderful price."
—Warren Buffett

A common mistake first-time rental property owners make is that they can adopt a completely hands-off approach. As long as the rent is getting paid and no one is actively complaining about anything, they don't want to be bothered. They don't even want to visit their own buildings if they don't have to. They don't want to go to meetings with other owners or the HOA.

The problem with the hands-off approach is that it leaves you blind to all the problems that might be brewing until they become major issues that could have been prevented with a little more awareness. By not taking an active role in your buildings, you won't know if your tenant is having an unapproved guest living in their unit. You won't know if someone is keeping four dogs on the premises instead of the one they told you about. It's human nature that people will almost always try to squeeze as much personal advantage out of a situation as possible. Many will surprise you with how sneaky and tricky they can be. No matter how you set it up, rental properties are never a totally hands-off investment. Even if you hire a management company, you have to know what's going on.

For example, I once asked a little old Mexican lady living alone in one of my units how it was possible that she was using more water than everyone around her combined. Was she showering multiple times a day? Doing her whole extended family's laundry? She ignored my probing until I did a little sneaky investigating and saw employees of the Mexican restaurant across the street stopping by her unit to fill up huge jugs of water. It turned out she was using a special filter on the water and selling it by the gallon to the restaurant for them to use in their agua fresca and horchata drinks. Whatever she was using to filter it must have worked because they were known for their really good drinks. The only problem was that I was the one paying for the water!

Should apartment owners hire a property manager or manage it themselves? Well, that's the beauty of it. If you get in there and it's small enough, you can manage it yourself, have somebody act as your proxy, or hire somebody like a property management company to help manage it. It's good to get your hands dirty and understand the job well before you pass it along.

Rather than going with a major management company, you can also opt to privately hire a manager who lives onsite as one of your tenants as part of their compensation. However, just like with your regular tenants, you must ensure you adhere to fair housing laws and protect tenant privacy. You're not exempt from complying with local and state regulations.

A good resident manager needs to be a jack-of-all-trades, with a keen understanding of property management, customer service, and conflict resolution. You must clearly outline job responsibilities and expectations to avoid any misunderstandings. Training and support are crucial for your resident manager. You need to provide initial training and ongoing professional development opportunities.

Two common methods to pay a resident manager are rent deduction and W-2 employment. Rent deduction means that the resident manager lives onsite and has their rent deducted from their paycheck in exchange for performing management duties. This method can save you money on payroll taxes and gives the resident manager a place to live. Just make sure that the rent deduction amount is reasonable and does not result in the resident manager being paid less than minimum wage.

Alternatively, W-2 employment means that the resident manager is treated as an employee and is paid a regular salary or hourly wage. This method ensures compliance with labor laws and provides the resident manager with benefits such as workers' compensation and unemployment insurance. However, it can be more expensive than rent deduction due to payroll taxes and benefit costs. Carefully consider which method to use and consult with a professional, such as an accountant or attorney, to ensure compliance with all governing bodies, such as the Department of Real Estate and the Labor Board.

WORKING WITH PROPERTY MANAGEMENT COMPANIES

When working with property managers, it's imperative to sit down and discuss your objectives as the property owner and investor. They need to know what you want and how you want to get it. However, they typically don't ask you these questions. They follow the path of least resistance, which means keeping the rent and expenses to a minimum unless you go out of your way to instruct them differently.

When you interview property managers, they're going to say a lot of things to get you in the door, so think now about what kind of person you want to work with. Do you want a discount property broker who is never going to return your calls, who isn't going to be able to help you make informed decisions, but who is going to still get the job done? Or do you want somebody who's going to answer the phone when you call instead of delegating it to some second-, third-, or fourth-tier individual?

An attentive property manager will know what you want before hiring them. They will go out of their way to try and understand what all your objectives are. Do you want to improve the property more? To be positioning the asset to increase the value of the property? If so, how much are you comfortable spending on a property to get money out? Or are you the kind of person who's worked so hard to get this property that you want to get as much cash flow as you can? What level of engagement do you want in the management decisions of the property? Do you want the property manager to just send you a check every month? What about keeping you informed of the ongoings of the property?

One property we purchased came to us with an existing onsite manager. He was a nice enough fellow who tried his best to make people happy. This turned out to be his fatal flaw, though. After some time of thinking he was doing a great job of managing the property and keeping the residents happy, we found out that he had been allowing several homeless individuals to reside in the laundry room during off hours. We had to ask him to stop doing this for our residents' security and the building's cleanliness. Though he nodded his head and agreed, he didn't stop. So, sometimes, even experienced property managers can do things that harm the functioning of your property.

Ask yourself these kinds of questions now. Do you plan on holding the property for 100 years? Or do you plan on holding it for only three years and want to increase its value before then? Is your property manager willing to put in the time to deal with increased vacancy factors and increased construction costs?

The more time and energy a property management company has to spend on you, the more money they're going to charge you. I would rather pay more for a property manager and know that they are really pushing through my objectives and helping to increase the value of an asset. I would much rather hire a property manager who's got millions of dollars of assets under their stewardship, knowing that they do a good job. I would not want to hire a property manager who doesn't own anything and who would be looking at it as just another job. Vetting property managers and management companies is, in some ways, a bigger necessity than vetting real estate agents or brokers. You have only a 60-to-90-day relationship with them.

You want to look at somebody who's invested in continuing education and ensure that they are at the precipice of new developments. You don't want to end up with a little old family-run management company that doesn't do any modern educational training. They might not know, for instance, the changing legal criteria that dictate when you can and cannot evict certain people in case it ever becomes necessary. If your property manager hasn't paid attention to changing laws in 10, 20, or 30 years, you're going to suffer because of it. You are basically trusting someone else to steward your largest asset and handle it properly.

Property management fees are generally based on a percentage of the property's revenue, with some established minimum. This includes all sources of income besides just the monthly rent, such as parking fees and other paid amenities. The property management company usually takes 3% to 7% of that effective gross revenue. The amount can change depending on the size of the property and its particular management requirements. Generally, the smaller properties with fewer units will carry a higher percentage fee. The larger the property or the more units it has, the lower the percentage. You'll also be responsible for paying the salaries of the staff managed by the company, which is not included in their percentage.

That percentage paid should cover most aspects of the service the property management company provides for you. However, it's best to read through your management agreement and make sure to take note of further additional fees, which may include other admin fees, hard costs, construction management, etc. This includes bookkeeping, third-party services, staffing, and financial reporting beyond the day-to-day tasks of reviewing the property. What's left for you as the owner are mostly the strategic decisions and renovations. However, the property management company may also want to handle renovations or maintenance because it can negatively affect them if the work is done improperly or is not up to code.

Your property manager will probably handle the leasing with each tenant, as they tend to be pretty standard across the board with multi-family properties (e.g., identical language, time period, and conditions for all tenants). There's usually little reason for the owner to come in and personally negotiate special conditions with individual tenants. Keep in mind that this does not include the on-site manager fee (if the property requires it by law), usually at 16+ units.

I almost always recommend that new owners find a reputable property management company and let them stabilize the asset. Still, many people don't want to pay a property management company 3% to 7% of their gross income for something they think they could easily do themselves. What a good management company does is keep an eye on your assets at all times for you. They make sure that there isn't mold. They make sure the toilets don't run. They make sure the residents are satisfied and free up your time and stress tolerance from dealing with their complaints. They let you live your own life and reap the lifestyle benefits of being a good investor.

Again, I ask: What is the opportunity cost of your life? Even though I now own a property management company, I love delegating the main functions (everything but the highest-level decisions) to others. Why do I do that? Because I want to be free to live my life. I want to do whatever I want and go on my way. This is why I've set up systems and procedures that leave me mostly free to set my own schedule and enjoy my freedom.

MANAGING THE PROPERTY YOURSELF

If you're more hands-on, you may not like the idea of leaving your property in someone else's care. Though I prefer using a management company for all my properties, some investors still want to manage their properties themselves. I've tried this many times in the past, and I've learned it's simply not for me. But it could be a good fit for you, depending on your personality and availability. Managing your property on your own means that you'll need to be more intensive than you would otherwise have to be.

Many tools are available to lessen the burden of managing your own property. Find online software that specializes in residential management. They will help you keep ACH or automated rent payments and maintenance requests in one place. Take the time to purchase and install cameras at various locations throughout your property to keep an eye on things from anywhere you happen to be. In fact, in California, you only need a manager physically there if your property exceeds 16 units. Join apartment associations to be kept abreast of current laws, documentation, and preferred vendors for recurring needs at the property.

It's a good idea to learn the ebbs and flows of the tenants at a property and time your presence there around them. Most new investors will start with something small, like fewer than ten units. But even at that scale, there are enough tenants to take up all your time if you let them. They're going to want to talk to you about their day. They're going to complain about various issues with the building. It's a major impediment to you just trying to get in, get your various tasks done, and move on.

How you interact with your tenants is ultimately up to you. But know that if you do make small talk with them, they will start to feel that they can dump many of their problems on you. Sometimes, you are expected to act as a psychiatrist to them. Sometimes, they want extensions on their rent payments. I don't even like making eye contact with people when I visit my properties because I don't want them to bother me five times a day. Waving creates the impression that you're someone approachable. I'd rather pay someone else to fill that role for me because it is still a necessary part of maintaining good tenant relationships.

I have found that it's a good idea to keep a neutral position with my residents. I've learned not to make too much eye contact with tenants unless I need to interact directly with them for some reason. I drive a nondescript car and dress casually. Occasionally, I've spoken Spanish and acted like I'm from another country to avoid getting sidetracked by talkative tenants. Sometimes, I'll have a gardening tool in hand so I can create the impression that I am busy and on my way to an important gardening task.

If you collect rent payments in person, you can become a target for theft. If tenants know when you will be present and carrying large amounts of cash, they could tell someone willing to take it from you by force. Fortunately, you can use plenty of affordable property management software to collect e-payments, deal with maintenance requests, and keep it all above board. If you don't have records of all these things, you're opening yourself up to big long-term tenant problems.

I like to regularly walk through my properties and do spot checks for indicators that problems may arise soon so I can address them before they grow bigger. The other day, I saw two front lights near the face of my building in the middle of the day. This informs me that I need to check these things more closely because those lights should already be on a timer that automatically turns them off during the day.

What else might I see during my daily walkabouts? A bit of trash strewn about in common areas. Cigarette butts, gum wrappers, and soda cans in the front yard. This informs me that my landscaper isn't doing their job. If you don't have an onsite manager at a smaller property, these duties fall under the purview of the maintenance supervisor and/or landscaper. This is just another good reason to buy property that is close enough for you to easily access. It's the only way to make sure it's being managed the way you want.

So, whether you manage your property yourself or have someone else manage it for you, it makes sense to have some kind of regular schedule for visiting and inspecting your property. Walk around your property every month or quarter to see if people are leaving possessions out in common areas. See if people are growing plants where they shouldn't be. See if the trash cans have been taken in, if there's graffiti anywhere, if any pipes are leaking, if dogs are barking, and so forth. I like to have all my buildings be pet-friendly, partially to keep my tenants happy but also because I can charge a small premium for it. However, this also means having to check if there is ever dog poop in the courtyard.

Make sure you do sufficient inspections inside each individual unit. Even if it's just a studio or one-bedroom apartment, you might be surprised to find eight people staying there because they're just trying to survive and can't afford the high cost of rent on their own. When that happens, you are harboring unsafe conditions. If it's found out, you could be held liable. In most studios, you can't have more than two adults and one child. In most one-bedrooms, you can't have more than three adults and two children.

As well, there's the increased utility load to consider. Keep in mind benchmarks of common utility loads for similar-sized units with similar occupancy. If the water bill is excessively large in one unit, it could be due to plumbing leaks or more people showering and flushing than there should be. It might behoove you to put a brick in the toilet tank so it uses less water or get water-efficient toilets installed to save you money in the long run. It also makes sense to put in aerated shower heads and sink faucets. They use less water but still perform their function well. Children use more water than adults because they don't turn off the water when they are done using it. If the tenant pays for utilities, average consumption drops by 30%.

Put filters in the shower drains to catch hair before it becomes an expensive clog. Some residents have a lot of hair. Some tenants put gunk into showers or toilets that shouldn't be there, such as sanitary napkins, tampons, or diapers. You should put a clause in your rental contract that states any expenses incurred get billed to the tenant.

On any given day of managing your properties, it's impossible to say what might happen. There really is no such thing as a typical day in this domain. A tenant will lock themselves out of their unit. A valuable package will disappear from the premises. Was it a thief? More likely, someone careless just misplaced it. Maybe you'll be notified that the unit subflooring caved in, and you need to replace the bathtub. If you're lucky, nobody will have been hurt. Or maybe your construction crew finds a wasp's nest in a torn-out wall that requires specialists to come in and remove it properly. Random leaks or black mold can show up out of nowhere.

On one of my daily checkups at an old 1920s construction containing six different cottages on a shared parcel, one resident decided to create a particularly intrusive scene. This woman hadn't been able to pay her rent for some time and grew increasingly violent and vocal about it. When the day came to finally evict her, this 6"1' 300-pound woman decided to answer the door to her unit completely naked and reeking of unwashed body odor. "Yeah, what do you want?" she asked in a dismissive tone. The sheriff who was with us to enforce the eviction stood stupefied at this presentation. He turned to his radio. "Uh... yeah... we're gonna need a female sheriff here immediately."

So there we stood, on that scorching day, for about 20 minutes. Finally, this 5"2' 100-pound blonde female officer with a ponytail showed up to put our naked evictee in handcuffs and escort her out of the unit. The sight of the size difference between them made for one of my most memorable days on the job. It was uncomfortable to watch, but sometimes you've got to appreciate and respect law enforcement's role. I did not want to think about an altercation or allegations of impropriety that could have happened if I had dealt with the situation alone.

At one of my 30-unit apartment buildings, an unexpected incident with a resident occurred on the fire escape of the third floor. A strange little fellow who lived in one of that floor's units had cupped his hands over his mouth and yelled to us, "Woo hoo! Woo hoo! I'll give you a good time for $50!" He flamboyantly waved a handkerchief at us to ensure we were looking at him. We learned that he had been performing oral sex for money out of his apartment. Wait, though; it gets worse. He was also a member of HOPWA: House Opportunities for Persons with AIDS, which is a federal program dedicated to helping people with HIV/AIDS find housing. So you can imagine the public health safety risk he posed by doing what he did.

CHAPTER 10

THE KEY TO GOOD TENANT RELATIONS: COMMUNICATION AND PROBLEM-SOLVING

"Communication is the fuel that keeps the fire of your relationship burning. Without it, your relationship goes cold."
—William Paisley

Finding new tenants to fill vacancies is a constant task for the multifamily property owner. There are many avenues one can pursue to find new tenants. You can look at sites like Zillow and Zumper. You can put a "for rent" sign in front of the property. You can place ads in newspapers. You can go to real estate exchanges or associations. You can have real estate agents put your vacancies on a Multiple Listings Service or other digital advertising forum.

A better channel for finding good tenants than most owners realize is simple word of mouth. If you own an apartment building, you can let other people know that there's a vacancy coming up, and you'll be giving a slight discount. I'll even let my existing tenants know that I have a unit that's about to become available. If they can find someone to occupy it (usually a friend or family member who has been looking for a place to live), I give them $100 and $100 off the new tenant's first month of rent. That gets family members and friends living next to each other, which means they're far less likely to move out because of the social ties they have in my building. It's a win/win because they also have a higher quality of life.

Most of the potential problems that can arise in tenant relations can be avoided by how you screen and select tenants in the first place. But the question remains: How do you differentiate a so-called "good" tenant from a "bad" one? Finding the right tenants makes your experience as the property owner substantially easier and more pleasant because you will have the peace of mind that they will pay when they are supposed to. You will go to sleep at night with confidence that they will respect your property. They will communicate openly with you about important matters that affect your investment and their satisfaction.

While you might be tempted to default to the most visible elements of what seems to make a person organized, respectful, and trustworthy (such as the way they dress or the type of car they drive), these superficial indicators usually end up mattering a lot less than some other core attributes. Your main concern should be whether the person you allow to come to live in your property will be a steady and reliable tenant who stays long, always pays on time, and causes minimal trouble with you or other tenants. This can come down to whether they have a steady job or not. It can be related to whether they have lots of close friends or family in the area.

How long did they stay at their previous place of residence? And how long have they been at their job? How many references do they have, and do they seem authoritative to you (such as someone in a position of professional or social importance), or is it just their buddy saying nice things about them?

If applicants relate tales of past experiences with landlords or property management, it can reveal your future with them as your tenants. Does it seem clear to you that the applicant may have been in some way a part of the problem and made resolving it much more difficult? Or is their transparency about past issues actually a good thing? It could indicate that they are good communicators and will work with you to swiftly resolve problems when they arise. A call to their previous property manager for reference can help you better understand the situation.

HOW DO YOU BUILD AND MAINTAIN GOOD TENANT RELATIONS?

There's a negative stereotypical trope that the relationship between tenants and landlords is often tenuous and adversarial. What you have to understand is that rent is usually the largest regular expense that a tenant is going to be paying. It encompasses 40% or more of their income in most cases. This obligation can lead to resentment and the perception of certain obligations from the tenant.

Conversely, the landlord can have their own reasons for being at arms with a tenant, which could include excessive amounts of complaints from them or requests for improvements to the property. Clogged toilets, broken keys, and dog poop filling up the yard could incense anyone with resentment. Maintaining basic health and safety standards on your property (which is a clause that should be explicitly included in the lease) is part of the tenants' obligation to you. Or maybe the tenant just can't pay their rent for an extended period of time due to personal problems.

A great deal of this potential conflict between tenants and landlords can be mitigated by recruiting tenants of good temperament and with whom you can build genuinely good relationships. There doesn't need to be a conflict of interest between you. Having a good property manager with excellent people skills goes a long way, too.

As an owner or as a property manager, you've got to be somewhat of a therapist in some cases when tenant disputes arise. You have to operate with a level of respect and open communication and help proactively solve problems so that you keep your tenants satisfied. When tenants are unsatisfied, they can always exercise their right to move out. Then, you will be stuck with vacancies and will have to put money into bringing that unit's condition back to what it should be and finding someone new.

Good tenant relationships are about open communication and respect. If somebody has a problem and you're able to address it, you often don't even need to solve the problem so long as the tenant sees that you are taking their complaint seriously and acknowledging their concerns. Some people just want to feel respected and heard, even if it's not actually in your power or budget to do anything about it.

A tenant of mine once bought an electric car and requested that I put an electric charger in a building built in 1929. I would have had to redo all the electrical to do that, as everything was running on fuses instead of circuit breakers. That would have cost me somewhere between $10,000 and $30,000. It simply wasn't an equitable decision, no matter what angle I looked at it from. I listened to them and explained the situation, showing that I was empathetic to their needs but would be unable to help in this particular case. They understood, and we maintained a healthy relationship for many years to come after that.

An example of a situation where I was able to do something to improve my relationship with clients and alleviate their complaints was during the COVID-19 lockdowns in 2020. Based on general feedback I received from many of my tenants, I decided to put Wi-Fi and a Wi-Fi mesh extender throughout the whole building to be able to provide free Wi-Fi to everyone during a time when people were spending much more time at home and on-line. Many of them had not bothered to or could not afford their own internet connection. This way, everyone had a better time remaining in my units and developed a much stronger opinion of me and the property. That was a benefit that was passed on to them free of charge to increase tenant satisfaction for a nominal cost to me while keeping up good relations.

Soon, I'm going to be raising the rent on many of my long-term tenants. By doing this, I risk pricing them out of the market and forcing them to leave to live somewhere cheaper. And even if they stay, I risk worsening my relationship with them if they hold a grudge against me for changing the price after they'd gotten used to it being lower. However, if I don't raise the rent,, I'll be operating at a loss because the value of the dollar has gone down through currency debasement and inflationary factors. I have to keep up with inflation to stay in business. My goal is to be able to offer the best deal that the economy will allow to my tenants and keep them happy with their choice to remain housed under me. That means I have to operate in a way that allows me to stay in business. However, I believe the least I can do in this situation is to make the transition as easy as possible on renewing tenants by informing them of the changing conditions long before it comes time to sign a new lease with different terms. They should feel fully informed and prepared to make the choice of either staying here under the new pricing or moving elsewhere.

Unlike the rental leases for most office spaces and commercial properties, multifamily rental terms are usually uniform across the board for all tenants. They are much shorter lease terms, usually 6 to 18 months instead of a few years or longer (or even month-to-month). After that, the tenant either renews their lease with updated terms or automatically reverts to month-to-month. Otherwise, they have to find somewhere else to live, in which case you would seek to fill the unit with a new tenant. This constant cycle of renewal or re-placement makes multifamily properties particularly sensitive to changes in the rental market. Your tenants are in a frequent position to re-assess whether they are getting a favorable deal by renting from you or whether they'd rather take their business elsewhere.

Your goal, of course, is to be able to raise rents as much as the market conditions allow for by offering a better place to live than what is currently available in the same area. But market rental rates can also drop between lease renewals for reasons beyond your control. As the property owner and investor, you need to be conscious of these developments. With the reduced security deposits and variability of financial means in short periods, a sound decision to move a qualified resident in could quickly turn into a less-than-ideal scenario if that resident loses their job or has a family concern requiring them to move. However, if they are small enough, remodeling and renting the properties out fairly quickly is easy.

DEALING WITH PROBLEMATIC TENANTS

My take is that there are no bad tenants, only bad communication. Yes, I have had tenants arrested. Yes, I have had tenants offering to perform oral sex for $50 off the rent. Yes, I have had tenants who paid their entire month's rent in $1 bills (don't ask where they got them from). Yes, I have had tenants who have stabbed other tenants on the premises of my property. Yes, I have had tenants who have committed suicide in my units. Yes, I've had tenants doing and dealing illegal drugs in my units.

But each of these unpleasant instances and any others you can think of are examples of failing to build the appropriate relationship and rapport with the people I was renting my units to. I failed to understand their needs and figure out a proactive way to solve these conflicts before they became major problems. And in cases where there was no solution, I failed to effectively screen those tenants out from entering my units in the first place.

I would even go so far as to say that tenants who damage property or need to be evicted are not necessarily bad tenants either. They face their own personal hurdles and obstacles, and they haven't been properly educated about right or wrong or how they should act. If communication fails, though, and there's nothing else reasonable you can do to fix the issue, eviction becomes a necessity.

Many times, when a tenant ends up damaging their unit, we don't actually find out about it until after they move out because we're not doing continuous active inspections in every unit. Maybe someone punched a hole in the drywall and put a piece of art in front of it, so we miss it while they are still there. Of course, we try to pay for the damage from the security deposit if sufficient funds exist. But if necessary, we can also take them to small claims court, get a judgment, tarnish their credit, and even garnish their wages.

I stress to all my tenants the need to communicate well with the property manager or me. Without communication, we don't know what's going on. We don't know if you have a problem with something in your unit or with something one of your neighbors is doing to disturb you. And eventually, these small issues, unaddressed, turn into big issues.

One time, I actually had a resident get stabbed at one of my properties. No matter how secure you try to make your properties, unfortunate things like this happen if you're in the game long enough. In this case, the victim didn't want to get the police involved. However, our hands were tied. It'd have been a big liability to the rest of the tenants to ignore this event and not inform law enforcement. The injured tenant was upset with us for calling the police, but he didn't realize the ramifications on the entire building. The fact that someone has been on the property stabbing somebody, whether it was a personal dispute between them or not, could put other people at risk.

I was once notified by a district attorney that I had to evict a tenant. In my perspective, the tenant was paying their rent and doing everything right, but the district attorney alleged that this resident was running a meth lab in our unit. Even though I could not directly verify these claims, I was obligated to listen to the DA.

I have a resident who likes to host parties in the common area without asking other tenants if they mind. She'll set up chairs and blast party music. She will put carnitas in a pot out in front, which means boiling water with pig entrails and pork meat. It's delicious, but it's dangerous, and it's against the health code. Then, she leaves the leftovers in the trash, which attracts raccoons, possums, and dogs. Preventative actions are the key here. Ensure your residents understand they can't be having a swap meet at the front of your property or hosting parties.

The bottom line is that every landlord needs to be aware of incompatible tenant behaviors that could arise and either need to be addressed and rectified immediately or turn into evictions soon if rectification is not possible.

So, how do you work to best make your tenants aware of the required standards inside and outside the units they rent? What about those who just flat-out refuse to cooperate and get along?

Reasonable expectations of behavior should always be outlined in the tenant lease, including clauses that specifically address how the tenant is required and expected to maintain the cleanliness of their unit, use appliances properly, allow other people into their units, maintain a reasonable level of noise, and interact with tenants occupying other units. This will reduce the chances of inter-tenant disputes, maintenance costs you will incur as landlord, and tenant turnover rate.

As well, you will learn to develop an effective vetting process for weeding out people who are likely to be problematic before they ever become your tenants. How do you determine who will be the most respectful tenants? Who will follow the rules they have agreed to and pay their rent on time?

Taking the time to vet and choose the best tenants will make your life as a rental property owner substantially easier in the long run. The best tenants are those who will respect you, respect each other, and respect the agreements they've made about how they will treat your property. The burden is on you to determine if they are responsible enough to meet these criteria.

Subjective judgments of appearance might seem like a good place to start this analysis, but they hardly tell the full story of a tenant. Sure, having nice clothes and a clean car might indicate that they are tidy, but maybe they have external reasons to keep those things clean that won't necessarily apply to their private lives at home. Better indicators of reliability would be things like a history of a stable job or having previously stayed in one apartment for a long time. Still, none of these can ever offer a complete picture. This is why personal references can be so important, particularly references from former landlords who can tell you if they have a history of problematic behavior.

Of course, it goes without saying that a record of violent or antisocial criminal behavior should be a major red flag to any property owner considering letting someone live in one of their units close to others. But not all criminal behavior is equal, and minor mistakes made long ago in the past do not usually reflect on the caliber of the person you are dealing with in the present. At the end of that day, you have to trust your gut and intuition before handing over the keys to one of your units.

A big problem emerges when tenants don't see that their unclean behavior is more than just an aesthetic issue. It also causes expensive damage that you have to pay for. Food left out attracts infestation. Reckless behavior causes broken windows, scuffed floors, holes in drywall, and structural damage. You can avoid most of these problems by vetting prospective tenants well and outlining expected hygiene standards in your lease agreements. But when the time comes that you need to address an issue with an unclean tenant, there are steps you can take to make the process easier.

SIX TYPES OF PROBLEM TENANTS

You'll encounter six types of problem tenants as a property owner.

First, there are late or partially paying tenants who almost always find difficulty paying rent by the due date. There are rare times when leeway can be given if you can manage to give it. But these tenants seek aid consistently, which can cause problems with your management and payroll. The most viable solution is to establish a firm policy of late fees any time the full rent is not paid on time. Otherwise, a non-payment of rent notice and the threat of eviction will become a soul-crushing, endlessly recurring theme.

Be wary of the rare tenant who will make it a personal mission to complain about every little thing. These types will inundate others with unreasonable requests, going far beyond tenants with legitimate repair requests. Any time something appears to be working but may be slightly wrong, even if it's been checked out multiple times, these types of residents will find a way to notify you. If you see this pattern emerging with a tenant, nip it in the bud. Establish clear guidelines on how they may contact you with a perceived problem.

Pet-friendly properties are a great way to attract tenants and increase your income. Some pet owners may push this too far, however. Pet hair gets everywhere (and maybe can't be cleaned out). Dogs chew on things, sometimes other residents' animals. Cats knock glasses off tables or miss the litter box. These can be expensive problems, making renting out the unit to the next tenant harder. Do additional inspections on units with pets in them to prevent this from happening with indulgent pet owners. Some tenants may attempt to bring their pets in without informing you, which is obviously not okay.

"Bulls in a China shop" are residents prone to repeatedly causing significant property damage. Excessive photographic documentation is your best friend here, as it makes it much easier to prove a unit's condition during your inspections. This makes it much more likely you will be able to get your tenant to pay for the damages they cause (if they can't fix them themselves), and it will disincentivize them from doing it again. Yes, this can even apply to "improvements" the tenant makes without your approval, such as painting the walls an extravagant color or adding fixtures to the wall. These can lower the value of the unit for the next tenant, so the current tenant should be expected to revert everything back to how it was before they leave. Wrecking balls who won't fix or pay for the damage they cause should be notified of impending eviction if they don't comply within a certain timeframe.

Then, there is the type of tenant who will constantly bring guests in to stay long-term in their unit without your approval. Some are just friends who don't leave for a long time, while others may be people the tenant brought in to sublet part of their unit. I call them "hosts to all." It can be a major problem because it means a constant influx of new people you didn't screen and approve of occupying the unit and shared areas. The best protection against this is clearly outlining in your lease agreement the circumstances under which guests can stay in a unit (and for how long). If someone else is moving in long term, you should also screen them, and additional fees should apply.

Finally, possibly the worst type of problem tenant to deal with is the lawbreaker. The number of creative ways that some tenants find to break the law in their units never ceases to amaze me. They might be growing, making, storing, and/or selling drugs there. They might be operating as prostitutes and bringing clients into their rooms. They could be professional thieves who bring their stolen goods back home with them. In all these cases, eviction is usually the proper course of action. You may even need to get the police involved if the crime is serious enough and puts others at risk. A good background check will pick up someone's criminal record if they have one, but there's always the possibility of renting to a criminal with a clean record.

Regardless, some amount of conflict with tenants will always be inevitable. Therefore, you need a viable way of nullifying it and maintaining good relations with the tenants to the extent that it is possible. If it is not possible or inordinately difficult, eviction may be the only alternative.

Clear and accurate communication is always the key. It might start with a private casual conversation with the uncooperative tenant where you let them know they've not been fulfilling their obligations. This leads to documentation of the problem behaviors if they are not changed, followed by a formal letter that informs the tenant of what actions they can expect to be taken if the problem is not solved. The sooner you begin this process and the clearer you make your grievances, the better chance you have of getting the problem solved before it grows unmanageable or the tenant becomes unreasonable.

The tenant may not even know they've violated a rule or why it matters, so be prepared to explain it calmly but firmly. Health and safety violations are important matters, as are protecting the value of your investment and respecting the peace of your neighbors.

If the time comes to document the problem, take detailed photos of the offending behavior from multiple angles with dates and times. Keep records of all communication about the matter, including calls and emails. The last step is a formal written notice, which is usually approved by a lawyer so that the language is clear and legally binding. The notice should mention the specific clauses of the lease agreement that have been violated. It should provide a deadline by which the problems must be corrected and what the consequences for not doing so will be.

It's pertinent to send out rent invoices a week before the first of the month and, if not paid within the stated grace period, notify promptly about late fees. This will, more often than not, help communicate to the resident the expectations that come with the property. If these simple actions aren't adhered to, a landlord or property management company will face countless unnecessary hassles.

Simple maintenance requests can also get out of hand if not pre-sorted on the phone prior to spending the time and energy to send someone out. After a few simple questions, it can be determined if the tenant caused the damage. If so, there will be the expectation and communication that they will need to pay for the work once completed. Operating in this approach will mitigate the chances of tenants taking advantage of the system and not paying for damages they cause to your units.

On one property, we inherited the onsite manager from the previous owner. He was a nice enough fellow who didn't really create much conflict and tried to make people happy. This seemed to be fine at first. However, we eventually discovered that he allowed homeless people to reside in the laundry room during off hours. For the security of our paying residents and the cleanliness and stewardship of the building, we had to ask the onsite to stop doing this. Though he nodded his head and agreed, he didn't stop letting homeless people crash in the common areas. We ended up having to fire and replace him.

INEVITABLE COLLISION: BAD DEBT, NON-PAYING TENANTS, AND EVICTIONS

It's important to be prepared for the possibility of bad debt and non-paying tenants. While it may seem daunting, the good news is that eviction is typically a last resort and can be avoided through open communication and proactive problem-solving. Additionally, it's important to note that the rate of tenants who fail to pay their rent tends to be lower in more expensive properties, as residents in Class A properties are more likely to have multiple sources of income and savings.

When it comes to collecting bad debt, options such as wage garnishment can be pursued. However, it's important to remember that this assumes the tenant has a job with wages to be garnished. If they don't, other options may need to be considered.

Evictions, while an unfortunate reality, can also be handled effectively with the help of a property management company. Typically, an eviction can take anywhere from one to three months. But with the help of a property management company, the process can be handled smoothly and efficiently. In the scope of operating your burgeoning apartment building empire, you will sooner or later face times when you and residents don't quite see eye to eye. The unfortunate experience of dealing with an eviction most often comes from the purchase of a property and the inheriting of a resident who is used to things operating in a different way. The previous owner may also have onboarded residents who normally wouldn't qualify under your onboarding standards for easily identifiable reasons.

The COVID-19 pandemic brought eviction moratoriums, which prevented landlords from evicting tenants for failing to pay rent. However, this also meant that tenants were able to build up large amounts of debt without consequence. One resident in a 10-unit apartment building I owned didn't pay her rent for 12 months, building up a balance of about $20,000 that she owed us. When the time came that we were finally able to legally remove her from the unit, we had to go through the court system to have a three-day notice served on the door. Then, we had to wait for the court system to give a ruling unless the tenant wanted to go to court to fight the ruling for the eviction. Finally, the sheriffs showed up to open the door and forced the residents to pack their things and leave while the sheriffs were standing there.

Typically, an eviction can take from one to three months. However, due to COVID delays, we looked at more like four or five months. Unfortunately, there's nothing I can do on my own. Even if the resident is not there and I so much as open the door, that could violate the terms of our agreement.

From an investor's perspective, eviction moratoriums can impact their ability to collect rent and potentially maintain the financial viability of the investment. Property owners might face more than just the risk of rent moratoriums in challenging times. Tenants, faced with financial hardships, might attempt to exploit various circumstances to their advantage. This could include trying to break leases prematurely, refusing to pay rent, or seeking rent reductions, not necessarily out of genuine necessity but to navigate their own financial crunch.

Even those who are usually upright might feel compelled to take such actions when backed into a corner by crises, perceiving it as a zero-sum game for their family's welfare. As landlords, understanding this potential behavior can help in crafting effective management strategies. Landlords need to be aware of and comply with any eviction moratoriums in place, as violating them can result in legal consequences. It is also important for landlords to be aware of their rights and options under the moratoriums, such as seeking payment from tenants or assistance through government programs.

In the process of eviction, the landlord files a lawsuit called an unlawful detainer. A California landlord is prohibited from using any self-help measures and must take his case through the court process of unlawful detainer before unwilling tenants can be expelled. Tenants are allowed to present a variety of different defenses, including arguing that the landlord is retaliating against them for reporting code violations.

The tenant protections often mean that eviction cases take much longer than one might expect. Because of that, landlords can be willing to cede the tenants some extra time in the apartment or even give the tenants some financial assistance with moving expenses in exchange for their vacating the premises. Stipulated judgments work well in these cases since they can turn all of the agreed-upon terms between parties into an enforceable court order. A stipulated judgment can also be used in debt cases, where a creditor sues a debtor for nonpayment of debt and obtains a money judgment against the debtor. The creditor can then use various methods to collect the debt, including seizing the debtor's assets.

CHAPTER 11

BUILDING YOUR NET WORTH AND EXIT STRATEGIES

"Wealth is not about having a lot of money;
it's about having a lot of options."
—Chris Rock

Inflation? Sure, it's real. But for savvy real estate investors, it's not a buzz-kill—it's a golden opportunity. While others see rising prices and wring their hands, you see your real estate investments growing in value and rub yours together in anticipation. Real estate, in fact, thrives amid inflation. As property prices rise over time, your wealth expands right along with it. Inflation? You don't fear it. You've got real estate in your corner.

While it's true that other countries might be printing money at an even higher rate than the U.S., it just sweetens the deal for you. The U.S. dollar remains sturdy, often outpacing other currencies.

Economic challenges are real, but they're also your proving ground. They're where you, the audacious real estate investor, shine brightest. With your knowledge, your smarts, and your bold embrace of opportunity, you're not just surviving the financial waves—you're surfing them. Stay informed, stay strategic, and above all, stay optimistic. Your financial future is bright. Let's ride this wave together.

Equity is the difference between the valuation of a property and what you still owe against it. To increase equity quickly, aim to pay down the principal of your debt every month. A certain amount of your debt goes to interest, and the remainder goes to the principal. The principal reduces the balance so that you pay interest on the lower balance over time. However, if your rate is low and you can get a better return elsewhere, you've got to do the math and assess if this is the best path for you. On an adjustable or variable rate loan, any extra principal payments made will reduce the monthly payment at the rate adjustment, with the new payment calculated to pay off over the original term. The monthly payment will likely adjust if prior principal reduction payments have been made. This is because these types of loans are intended to continue for the entire length of the agreed-upon term, typically 30 years.

With biweekly loan payments, an extra payment each year pays the balance off faster. This method, when applied to your loan's principal, shaves approximately seven years off a 30-year fixed loan. Biweekly payments are half of your monthly payment, paid every two weeks. There are 52 weeks in a year or 26 biweekly payments. That equates to 13 full payments since an average month loosely comprises 4.3 weeks, not four exact weeks. Biweekly loan payments save money on interest by paying the loan down. When the principal balance is paid down faster, there's less money to charge interest on, lowering the overall cost. When the loan is paid off earlier, it shaves off several years' worth of interest payments.

You can also quickly increase your equity by strategically improving a property. At the time of this writing, I own a commercial space where I'm doing construction in the rear. I'm converting garages to be used for office space, and it's probably going to cost me $100,000 or so when all is said and done. The value of the property and the location is about $500 per square foot. However, once I convert one thousand square feet of garage into office space, it's going to increase the value of the property by about $500,000. I will spend $100,000 to make $500,000. The recapture period is the amount of time it takes to make the money back from improvements.

The longer you own a property, the more equity you'll be able to build in it. But another viable strategy is just to keep buying and exchanging, buying and exchanging, buying and exchanging instead of holding onto one property for a long time. You can actually build wealth quicker this way. It's a harder game requiring you to look at the return on equity. If you're 50% into a property and you have a 50% loan, you're not getting a very high return on equity. This might be okay if you prefer more stability and cash flow. But instead, you could use the bank's money at maybe 5% interest to go make more money. Try to find that sweet spot for return on equity. That depends on the economy, your personality, and your goals.

With a low return on equity, you're not using your assets optimally to make the most money possible. That is another way of saying there is a certain amount of money sitting in the property that you can't access. But if you can move the property, then you can borrow money with leverage. You can earn a greater return on your equity and get a higher cash-on-cash return by default. Understanding your return on equity helps you determine how well your property is performing.

PLANNING YOUR EXIT

Planning to exit a property with the highest amount of appreciation possible requires you to think strategically about how you added value to it while it was in your care. If you're able to convert a studio to a one-bedroom (and earn more monthly rental revenue in the process), you'll also have more money at the exit. If you do more inspections throughout the tenure of your ownership, you can defray many of the costs that pop up at the end when a buyer claims that their inspection shows that the property is in worse condition than they were told it was when they put in their offer. Suddenly, they've lowered their offer by $100,000 because of your negligence.

The first thing you want to do when you're ready to let go of your property is make sure that it's in the best physical condition it can be reasonably justified to be in. However, improving the condition could quickly become cost-prohibitive and is subject to interpretation among renters and owners. Optimal curb appeal is generally a good idea, though. Many simple wins, such as green and well-kept grass, not having residents' exterior furniture in the courtyard, keeping the concrete looking clean or wet, and organized parking, make a big difference. Pre-select which units you will walk through with the buyer in advance to ensure they look their best during inspection.

You also want it rented at the highest rate it can with the highest perceived cash flow. I say *perceived* cash flow because if you actually sold the property and then exchanged out, you would be able to get greater leverage with more of a loan. Then you'd have that cash to be buying more properties or a greater number of units. Then, you would be getting a greater cash flow with the increased leverage and higher cash-on-cash return.

At one property I was cleaning up and getting ready to sell, I found that three units needed new hardwood floors. We finished building them, and they turned out beautiful. The tenants loved them. However, I soon realized it was going to cost me $7,000 just to get somebody to polish them, finish them, and make them look as nice as possible. So that's an example of how what I thought was going to be a simple and relatively inexpensive aesthetic im- provement grew out of hand for me. I ultimately agreed to the $7,000 because it was a unique property that brought up the resplendent value of the past in a key location. Spending some money to enhance the value was a no-brainer.

One of the things that I'm coming to realize over the years is that I need to do inspections more often than I once thought, perhaps every six months to a year. I need to be more proactive about getting into each unit and closely examining what's going on. However, inspecting a unit is hard when people have their families and furniture everywhere. The couch or a cabinet may be hiding serious problems I need to know about, maybe things even the current tenant doesn't know about but should also be aware of for the sake of their health and safety. This is yet another reason to invest locally, within a phys- ical range you are comfortable regularly traveling: to keep your hand on the button and make sure the property is being serviced how you wish it to be.

You should frequently be checking if the fire extinguishers and smoke detectors are present and working. Take a look at all the plumbing. Make sure the sink is running and that the aerated nozzles are installed on the sink and shower to reduce the load of water. Make sure that nothing is leaking or running over. The last thing you want is to have leaks causing water damage that infiltrates into lower units.

Recently, after evicting a tenant who had occupied one of my units for more than three years, I finally had the opportunity to do a thorough inspection. We ended up finding all kinds of horrifying things that the tenants apparently weren't even aware of, such as black mold hidden inside the bathroom walls (which we only found by tearing them open) and an unsettled floor. Frankly, if they had gone to court with photos of the problems we found, the judge would have deemed it a warranty of habitability issue. It pains me to realize that I should have done more as the owner to be helping to protect those residents' rights, even if they didn't complain.

Warranty of habitability is a bundle of rights that residents have. They should have a roof over their head and walls that protect them from the elements. They should have heat and hot water. The unit should be free of contaminants like mold and asbestos. There should be no bug or rodent infestations. Plumbing, ventilation, and electrical should all be in working order. Tenants should not live in squalor, which is one of the implied promises landlords make merely by offering a place to live. Common areas like stairways and halls should also be clean and safe.

Breaching warranty of habitability is a potentially serious liability issue. That's what it's called when a landlord fails to meet these minimum requirements, which are part of the total bundle of tenant rights. It could either be the result of poor maintenance that causes something essential to fail, or perhaps the unit was never set up properly to begin with. In these cases, the tenant can attempt to sue the landlord. However, tenants can't build a case just because of some minor defect or inconvenience, as wear and damage in some regard are inevitable at every property. A breach of warranty of habitability is something major that renders the unit inhabitable. The only time this standard doesn't apply is when the tenant themselves is the one who damages the property and makes it uninhabitable, in which case they are obligated to repair or pay for it.

Tenants have rights under local, state, or federal law. Under the federal Fair Housing Act, tenants are not to be discriminated against based on factors like race, religion, gender, or sexual orientation. They have the right to not be charged excessively for a security deposit. No matter how cheap the rent on a place is and how low the expectations of quality are, these essentials must be guaranteed under threat of legal action. All tenants are entitled to a reasonable amount of privacy, meaning the landlord or management cannot barge into a unit even though they own it. When they need to access the unit for inspection or repairs, they are required to notify the tenant ahead of time.

In my situation, fixing those problems turned into an opportunity to upgrade and improve the other aspects of the unit. We tore out all of the drywall, redid the electrical, redid the plumbing, redid the bathrooms, and redid the kitchens. One of the biggest components of these renovations is paint. It's the cheapest thing to redo, and it gives the biggest visual effect for the tenant, improving their perception of quality. Another simple win is windows. The windows on that unit were old, but they didn't quite need to be replaced yet. Still, they didn't exactly make you feel like you were living at the Ritz. For $1,000, we got new windows in there, which made the next tenants feel like they were living somewhere much nicer. We also used this opportunity to make it a two-bedroom unit with built-in laundry and an open kitchen concept in the living room. This enabled us to increase the rental value from $1,495 to $2,195 per month with the same square footage. We ended up with much happier tenants, too.

BUILDING THE END INTO THE BEGINNING

The sale of one of my properties is usually strongly entwined with the conditions under which I purchased it. I know that if I buy the property at the wrong price, I'm not going to be able to sell it at the price I want. But if I buy something at the right price today, I know I will be able to sell it for a profit tomorrow. I look at the cash flow that the property provides and the gross income, among other metrics, to determine its accurate market value.

When entering a property, I ask myself several essential questions so that I won't be shooting myself in the foot when it comes time to exit. Do I know how long I plan to own the property? A two-year exit plan will look quite different from a ten-year exit plan (or longer). What do I plan to do with the proceeds from the sale? I might be involved in some very long-term plans to invest in a series of additional properties, or I might be planning my retirement. Do I want to hold onto the property for the long haul and even leave it to my kids? A clear understanding of the exit plan I want reduces stress for me and possible conflict among my partners.

Sometimes, selling is better just to make life easier and free up capital to put into something more worthwhile. If the amount you are earning from the property is not enough to justify the risk and time investment involved in the property, you'd probably be better off just putting the money somewhere safer and/or more passive. Sometimes, a loss in income or value can be anticipated ahead of time, such as if you predict too many apartments are going to be built in your area in the near future. This influx of supply will drive prices down, which means it might make sense for you to get out before that happens. The same reasoning can apply if you have a lot of expensive repairs and maintenance coming up and would rather pass that burden onto the new owner than deal with it yourself, so long as you don't mislead your buyer about the property's condition.

Has something major in your life changed recently? Maybe someone close to you passed away or someone new was born. Maybe a sudden expense popped up that would greatly benefit from liquidating one of your properties and freeing up your time. You invested in your property with certain long-term expectations of what would be going on in your life. If those circumstances suddenly change, it may warrant also changing your investment plan.

I once bought a 23-unit apartment property that came on the market for $1.6 million. I went in and raised the rent, which I justified by fixing up each unit. In nine months, I sold the property for $2.4 million. Could I have stayed and held it longer? Sure, but I was happy to walk away with $800,000 in eight months. I was able to take that and parlay it into another 20-unit building that I picked up for $1,122,000. After bringing up the rent and stabilizing the residency in eight months, I sold it for $1,550,000.

Typically, my exit plan involves stabilizing several units with a history of vacancy and renting them out at a higher level. Then, I'd add new paint, wainscoting, and molding on the doors. I like framing a kitchen, making the backsplash look good, and bringing in all-new stainless steel appliances. For the bathroom, I use hexagonal floor patterns, saving nozzles on all faucets, and I provide free Wi-Fi for the whole building because it saves my tenants a lot of cost and hassle.

Consider the enormous value that can be added to common areas and how it affects the perception of the person who will end up buying the property from you. For instance, I paid my gardener for a little co-op vegetable garden in one of my apartment buildings. Residents could come and tend to their own garden and harvest their veggies any time they wanted. By doing this, I was helping my residents enjoy the property more and giving them more space to do stuff with their free time. This means that they got more emotionally invested in living there, which means they were more reluctant to leave even if other issues arose. No one wants to just abandon the little tomato plant they've spent three months tending to.

Why is that important when it comes time to sell the property? Because if you're able to demonstrate a unique source of value for the residents, something that shows a greater pride of ownership, they will start to justify a higher purchasing price in their minds. The buyer knows that these little improvements will make it easier over the long run to raise rents, retain residents, and maintain good relationships all around compared to a similar property that lacks these things.

There are many other ways to add value that amount to one-time irregular costs. Yet, they can improve the property, raise rents, and substantially increase tenant quality of life for the life of the property. Some of these will be in common areas that all tenants share, and some will be within the individual units themselves.

The common areas will benefit from an upgraded lobby and leasing center, a park, a place to socialize and watch movies, or even the addition of a gym. Common area improvements can be even more important than private unit improvements, as some tenants might choose to stay in your building primarily because of the common amenities you offer. These areas are the most visible to the public and prospective tenants, so they do a lot to add to your curb appeal and public image. As well, these improvements tend to be more affordable overall because you only need to make them once for the whole building, not over and over again for each unit. The more tenants can do without ever having to leave your building, the more incentive they have to remain tenants there. Why bother paying for an expensive gym membership and having to find time out of your busy schedule to travel to and from there when there's already a fully-equipped fitness club where you live?

Many real estate brokers like to use pro forma rents or rents that the property could achieve in their view of a perfect world. From these increased rents, they then argue a proforma value of the potential worth of the building.

However, this is a highly biased analysis. One can cherry-pick rents in the low or high end of anything to support their argument. Even with the variation in rents, one could then cherry-pick the capitalization rates and/or gross rate multipliers for the properties, not to mention the unit configurations, square footage, and so on. What one buyer is willing to pay for one property could be completely different from what another buyer is willing to pay for another property with virtually identical comparables.

Before buying a property, I look at it from the price per unit and the price per square foot. I compare it across comparable properties. Of course, many different qualities could be considered comparable with other properties. Do you use the location? The year built? The configuration? The design? The number of units? Are eight studios the same as eight one-bedrooms? I do a little bit of mental math. I find the range that I can argue is reasonable to drive the price down to in a negotiation so I can get it for the lowest possible price. Then, I do the same thing to determine the highest reasonable price for it. My goal is to reasonably know how much I will make at the time of my exit before I buy it, even if I end up selling it in the same condition it's in when I buy it.

However, I also dislike buying properties where I can't add value. Adding value is one of the most important components of real estate investing. Buying property for value appreciation is a great complement to buying for cash flow potential, and I've focused on it for the last 25 years in this business. The most value-added potential can be found in properties that have been poorly managed. Perhaps the rents have not been at market levels, or a high element of deferred maintenance has existed. Maybe the owners did not think about how to create alternative income streams from the property.

When you are doing comparables, most interpretations of what something is worth are quite subjective. That's why there are professional appraisers to help bring in a more objective perspective. However, even appraisers might not be neutral, such as if they are hired by the bank and therefore incentivized to work the numbers in their favor. Sometimes, banks want to go out of their way to make the value of a property appear as low as possible so they can justify giving you a smaller loan. Should the appraiser put the vacancy rate at 5% instead of 3%? Do they use the estimated expenses from Marshall and Swift, which is a nationwide standard for determining expenses, or do they have their own proprietary method of determining expenses for a property that reduces the income, the net income, and, by default, the value of the property?

There are many different reasons an owner might feel ready to let go of their multi-family rental property. It could be one of the three D's (death, divorce, or destitution) that cause you to sell. Maybe you are getting a poor return on your equity, but the value of the asset has gone up so much that it would still be profitable to sell. Maybe there's another property you could put that money into that will give you a better return. It all depends on what your goals are. Do you want the freedom and peace of mind that comes from owning properties outright? Or do you want to be taking bigger risks and moving your money around to wherever it will be giving you the greatest possible bang for your buck?

If you planned things out from the time of your purchase, you should already have a pretty good idea about most of the pertinent elements to planning a good exit. This is especially important if you've invested with partners. You should all have been on the same page from the start. No one should keep holding onto a property for longer than they feel comfortable being responsible for managing it, but you also shouldn't haphazardly discard a property when it doesn't financially suit you to. Or maybe your goal is to leave the income-producing property in your family to generate wealth for future generations.

Of course, the best reason to sell any apartment building is simply that you have been unable to keep it sufficiently occupied and producing enough income to justify keeping it. Ownership objectives vary, but it also could be a desired "return on equity" to maximize cash flow and leverage. But this is a worst-case scenario. The point of this book has been to teach you how to make rental property investing bountiful for you. Still, no one is guaranteed a profit. Maybe you just got yourself into a bad deal or had unexpected lifestyle factors prevent you from doing everything you would have liked to have done. Maybe new taxes or regulations went into effect in your area that limit your options as a rental property owner. Maybe new damages have popped up that you're not inclined to repair. In such cases, it's in your interest to hand your investment property off to someone more interested in making the most of it.

CHAPTER 12

NAVIGATING TAXES, LEGALITIES, AND LIABILITY

"The difference between death and taxes is death doesn't get worse every time Congress meets."
—Will Rogers

This chapter is not meant to instruct you on how to file your taxes. It is meant to inform you about many but not all of the options for using tax write-offs to lower your tax liability from real estate. The number of ways you can file your taxes is endless, and with more knowledge, you can learn how best to claim and argue your potential tax savings. As the wise and learned philosopher Benjamin Franklin once stated, "A penny saved is a penny earned." Use this as a fun endeavor to save all those pennies, buy more buildings, and free up your time to use what life you have left and make the most of it!

Depreciating an asset gives you a large number of write-offs. If you are a highly-paid professional or make a lot of money, for which you must file a W2, or even if you are a small business owner, a lot of withholding must go to the federal government, upwards of 30% to 40%. But if you have write-offs that go against your adjusted gross income and if you have, let's say,

$200,000 in income from your work, and you're paying about 40% in taxes, then you have $80,000 withheld by Uncle Sam. However, owning a $2 million apartment building could benefit by having maybe $60,000 in tax write-offs against that $80,000.

If you make $200,000 per year, it puts you in the highest-income tax bracket. You're probably paying about 42% towards the federal and state governments for taxes, so about $85,000. If you get a $60,000 write-off from real estate, it goes against your $200,000 and puts you at $140,000 in adjusted growth income, which may lower your tax bracket to 35% or even lower if you're married. So, you are not only getting the write-off, but you're also going into potentially lower tax brackets. Because I own so many buildings, my tax write-offs make it so I hardly have to pay any taxes.

Depreciation is a pretty straightforward process with real estate. The federal government permits you to claim that the upkeep of a property is going to be a consistent thing year after year for a tax deduction. The IRS accepts that the property has a determinable useful life. As properties age and the roof gets tattered or a water heater bursts or paint needs to be redone, there will be consistent recurring improvements for a property. The federal government recognizes this, allowing you to depreciate the property's value.

Depreciation usually gets reported on Schedule E of Form 1040. However, Form 4562 might come into play for a property in the year it becomes a rental property. Renting out a residential property means reporting rental income on your personal taxes unless it is rented out for 15 or fewer days during the tax year (in which case you also can't deduct rental expenses). Owners can also deduct homeowners insurance and some property taxes.

To claim property depreciation, you have to be the owner of the property, with only a few exceptions, and it must be producing income. Can you determine the useful life of your property based on its type and age? The remaining useful life has to be more than one year. Fortunately, the IRS has standardized how to determine the useful life of a property. The useful life of residential rental property under the General Depreciation System (GDS) is 27.5 years. However, under the Alternative Depreciation System (ADS), also allowed by the IRS, it's a bit longer at 30 years, but the amount of depreciation you can claim each year isn't as high. For nonresidential properties, these numbers extend to 39 and 40 years, respectively. Once you select one of these systems, you're stuck with it for the total length of time you claim depreciation.

To calculate your property depreciation, you must first determine your cost basis, the initial value from which depreciation will be taken. You will want to get a professional real estate appraisal for rental properties. You can also add some qualified closing costs, including property taxes, transfer taxes, legal fees, utility installation services, title insurance, and property line surveys. Then, divide this amount by the property's useful life.

When it comes time to sell a property, the IRS determines the capital gains tax based on the cost basis minus the depreciation compared against the higher amount you sell it for (as opposed to the amount you happened to pay for it when you bought it), so you end up paying more. It's called depreciation recapture. This is still better than not claiming depreciation at all, though.

As a simple rule of thumb, there are two parts to the valuation of a property: The land and the improvement on it. In scarce areas that are in higher demand, the value of the land contributes to a greater amount of the total property value than in areas where there are many options for buying. In Long Beach, for instance, an area perpetually in high demand, the land typically contributes between 70% and 80% of the value of a property. That's an argument you can make with the IRS on how you determine the land value and how you determine the building value.

Every tax benefit that currently exists has been fought for and carved out by people who came before us to give us a chance at eliminating our legal burden. If you're not using all of the weapons in your arsenal, then you're leaving money on the table and sacrificing more of your freedom than you have to. If you aim to maximize your freedom and opportunities to pursue what you want in life, you owe it to yourself to put in the work required to keep as much of your hard-earned money as possible. Keep your money to spend on yourself, your family, your friends, and your passions and values to create the life you want.

If you buy a $275,000 investment property, you can accelerate the depreciation to 27 and a half years, which is the minimum amount of time that the government will allow you to depreciate. They will allow you to go up to 39 and a half years. You can get a $10,000-a-year write-off using depreciation if you want to go less. Now, that write-off will come back to bite you because it's going to lower your basis. Your basis is the value of the property you are into for tax purposes. If I buy it for $275,000 and take that $10,000 write-off, when I sell the property for $300,000, that's a $25,000 profit. If I take the $10,000 depreciation, the IRS will see it as a $35,000 profit. Then you can just 1031 exchange, buy something else, and carry over that reduced basis to a different property.

One of the benefits that your primary residence home does get you is a $250,000 federal exemption. If you buy it for $250,000 and sell it for $500,000, you can have that $250,000 tax-free (assuming you own the property for two years). Or, if you moved to a different property and owned it within the past five years, you can claim that income tax-free. If you're married, it can go up to $500,000 tax-free. That is one way to make the home make sense for you if you are able to buy it below market. Know that in the short term, you can get the $250,000 tax-free. Then, you can get a nest egg of money for an income-producing asset. That's one way to come up with a down payment when you want to buy a property.

Doctors, dentists, lawyers, and other highly paid professionals earn their income by billable hours. The opportunity cost of them stepping away from their $300-to-$600-per-hour profession is too great to go out and get into real estate. They would rather take the dime they know. That's why they don't often get into real estate as investors. Instead, they're guided by their CPAs to get into real estate for the tax benefit it derives so that they can offset all their $300,000-to-$500,000 income. Their CPA tells them they should buy an apartment building to avoid paying $100,000 to $200,000 in taxes. Then, they'll have this large write-off to help offset their income. I've bought many of my properties from dentists or doctors so busy in their trade that it became prohibitive for them to manage the properties.

Knowing how to extract the most from time and money helps amplify outsize returns. That's why investing in real estate can be better than investing all one's time and money into a time-intensive profession for life where you only make more money by sacrificing more hours. A more entrepreneurial approach is to use other people's time in the form of employees and vendors to help you. Use other people's money in the form of loans and lines of credit for outsized returns.

Whatever you seek to accomplish by investing in rental properties, its success will be affected by the quality of how you spend your time. Everyone in the world has the same 24 hours in a day, and everyone must choose how to manage the time trade-offs they face in pursuit of their goals. Some applications of our time only deliver quick, short-term goals for us, and others can lead to massive long-term gains that we won't immediately realize. Everyone, ultimately, has a value that they assign to an hour or a day of their time, but for most people, it's more of an intuitive feeling than a serious consideration of when they would be better off hiring someone to do something for them or taking a faster but more expensive option.

1031 TAX-DEFERRED EXCHANGE

As an investor, it's to your advantage to expand and diversify your real estate portfolio while minimizing losses and expenses, including capital gains tax. A tool at your disposal is the 1031 exchange, a legal mechanism that allows you to swap one like-kind asset for another. This strategy bypasses the traditional sales process and defers taxes into the future. To be eligible, you can transition from one asset class to another, such as from commercial to residential, utilizing the 1031 exchange. The 1031 exchange, also known as a like-kind exchange, enables investors to reinvest proceeds from a sale into a similar property without incurring capital gains tax as long as certain conditions are met.

Like-kind exchange is where you exchange real estate for other real estate of the same type. This way, the IRS does not make you recognize a gain or loss under IRS Code Section 1031. However, if you receive any property that is not of the same type (not "like-kind") or money, that portion of the exchange must be recognized as a gain and filed as such on your taxes. Generally, property is considered to be like-kind if it is of the same nature. This applies even if one is much newer or better quality than the other. Whether improved or not, real estate is almost always considered like-kind with other real estate within the US.

This frees up more of your capital to go into another property right away, which means you will be more flexible in moving from underperforming assets to more profitable ones or from properties that might be difficult for you to manage to much easier ones.

When you sell something, and you've made a gain, you can cash out and get a check that will have 40% to 50% of it withheld by Uncle Sam. You will have to file on your taxes that you received that money. As an example, let's say you make $100,000. The escrow company will send a 1099 that you have to file on your taxes. Then, when you file your taxes, you'll be paying the government a lot of money. Your tax base will be 30% to 50%, depending on your tax rate. So, from that $100,000, you will have to send between $30,000 and $50,000 to Uncle Sam when you file your tax return.

The escape route from a potential financial burden lies within IRS code 1031. Individuals elect to sell a property in a 1031 exchange—a strategy to defer tax. They then engage with what is called an accommodator, a neutral third party trusted with the funds from the sale. This term, accommodator, carries significant weight as it represents the entity responsible for handling the transaction's funds.

If sellers decide to withdraw some of the sale funds, they will receive a 1099 for that particular distribution, a transaction often referred to as "boot" on the distribution. The property being sold holds the title "downleg," and the properties intended for purchase are known as the upleg. Once the sale is complete, you have a 45-day window to inform your accommodator about your prospective upleg properties. Failure to identify these properties within this timeframe will result in tax obligations. Subsequently, you can designate up to three properties as your uplegs, as long as their collective purchase price meets or surpasses the selling price of the downleg.

Furthermore, following the 45-day identification period, you have an additional 135 days—totaling 180 days from the sale—to close on your upleg properties. If you do not manage to close on those properties within the 180-day period, the previously deferred tax liability returns. In such a scenario, you will receive the full distribution and subsequently be issued a 1099, indicating to the IRS that a significant tax payment is impending.

When you're ready to purchase a property, the accommodator wires the necessary funds to the escrow, which then disburses the funds to the property seller. This method ensures the continuance of your tax-deferred status, provided all conditions are met and maintained.

1031 exchanges help build net worth quickly because you are not taxed on the money after each exchange. You're continuing to grow, and grow, and grow. If you take a 30% to 50% hit from your equity in taxes after each sale, you won't be able to accrue and accumulate net worth easily. You'll have far less capital with which to pursue new property opportunities. If you compound that 30% to 50% that would have been taken, you're using what would've been tax dollars to make more money instead. You're getting larger cash in return for your investment. Instead of having five figures go to the IRS, it's going toward a down payment. The main benefit of a 1031 exchange is it allows you to take 100% of your equity to purchase a larger replacement property or multiple properties to grow your portfolio.

Remember that the properties you pinpoint for the exchange must meet the "like-kind" criteria. This term signifies that the properties should possess a similar nature or character, even though their grade or quality can differ. Essentially, a commercial property can be exchanged for another commercial property, and a residential rental property can be exchanged for another residential rental property. The like-kind rule is typically straightforward to navigate, especially in the realm of residential rental properties.

Another useful hack with the IRS is claiming an improvement over an expense. There is no black-and-white method on how to claim whether you put something in as an improvement or at an expense. By claiming an expense, you can get a 100% deduction in that tax year for it. If you claim an improvement, you will have a depreciated portion. Roughly speaking, improvements are activities that put a property in better condition, and maintenance is anything that keeps the property in its operating condition.

In the eyes of the IRS, capital improvement is typically when you fix something defective or flawed, create an addition on the property, increase the size or capacity of something, adapt it to a new type of use, replace a structural component, or rebuild something that has worn out. What the IRS thinks of as routine maintenance doesn't quite fit into the description under normal circumstances. Recurring activities like inspection, cleaning, replacing worn-out parts, testing, etc., that happen as a result of the normal use of the property aren't capital improvements. These are upkeep activities that the owner should have reasonably expected to be performing when they acquired the property.

Subsequently, there's a recent thing called cost segregation. If you incur a huge hit for the sale of one property and want to offset that greatly, you can pay a company to do cost segregation. Their job is to assign a value to each nail, each bolt, each screw, and every little piece that went into the development of your property. Then, you can claim that write-off in the tax year to frontload write-offs to offset gains.

You can even work with your CPA to consider gifting a property that has a large potential gain to a common good, like a university. This way, you can have your name on it and carry forth a public legacy. It's a great way to leave a legacy with someone's namesake while also getting the benefit of not having to pay taxes from decades upon decades of 1031 exchanging. If you're so wealthy that you need to donate massive amounts of money to lower your tax burden, you could do so by putting your name on a property as a legacy for the future.

DELAWARE STATUTORY TRUSTS (DST)

When faced with a conundrum as a property investor, you may find yourself reluctant to sell and face a considerable tax obligation while also feeling weary of the increasing responsibilities of property ownership. Perhaps your property management company isn't delivering on its promises, leading to a surge in your daily involvement. This can result in constant phone calls, handling unanticipated issues, or even incurring hefty bills for significant repairs. Suddenly, what was supposed to be a passive income stream is anything but.

This situation is further exacerbated for some owners when their property is an aging building with accumulated equity but requires consistent maintenance. As an investor, your goal remains to generate a return on your investment without operational burdens. This situation prompts a question: How can you return to being a passive investor? It's a challenging predicament that warrants careful consideration.

One option is to 1031 exchange your assets and equity into something called a Delaware Statutory Trust (DST) instead of another property. This tax deferral program potentially benefits rental property owners everywhere in America—not just Delaware, as the name implies. It's a legal trust that enables investors to sell their property and defer taxation by buying replacement property. It's a holding company that's under management, and it puts you in competition with various funds or hedge funds. This can be an especially good option if you are unable to find a suitable replacement property to exchange into.

With a DST, hundreds of other investors can put their assets together, giving you a piece of a billion-dollar or more asset. Doing this will give you a marquee property with higher occupancy and greater consistency. If prices go up with inflation, your appreciation will be 3% on average. With a billion-dollar asset, that's going to be a $30 million increase per year, just in the value of the property. If you split that with 499 owners, you're going to make $60,000.

Additionally, once your property is part of a DST, it will be managed by the top people who will ensure every possible dollar is squeezed from it. They will take a large portion of the income for their part. However, the benefit to you is that you can camp the money there for a few years, maybe even up to a decade. You can get a consistent return on your investment of 4% to 7%, with the peace of mind that when it does sell, the value of the assets will be worth more, and it will have cash flow. In fact, the monthly income could easily exceed what you originally had.

REAL ESTATE INVESTMENT TRUSTS (REITS)

Real Estate Investment Trusts (REITs) are a type of investment vehicle that allows individual investors to invest in a diversified portfolio of real estate assets. REITs offer investors the opportunity to access professional management and expertise, which can be particularly appealing for those who prefer a more hands-off approach to real estate investing.

One of the key benefits of investing in REITs is the ability to diversify your portfolio. By investing in a REIT, you can gain exposure to a variety of real estate asset classes, such as residential, commercial, industrial, and hospitality properties, without having to directly own and manage individual properties. This can help reduce risk and improve returns.

REITs are also required to pay out at least 90% of their taxable income to shareholders, making them an attractive option for income-seeking investors. This can provide a steady stream of income without the need for active management.

However, it is important to note that REITs, like any investment, come with risks. One key risk is the potential for changes in real estate values, which can affect the value of REIT investments. REITs may also be subject to interest rate risk, as changes in interest rates can affect the value of their assets.

Overall, REITs can be valuable for real estate investors who prefer a more hands-off approach. By investing in a REIT, you can gain access to professional management and expertise, diversify your portfolio, and generate income while minimizing the time and effort required to manage individual properties.

ENTERPRISE ZONES

Enterprise zones are designated areas where businesses and investors can receive various tax incentives and other benefits to encourage economic development and revitalization. These incentives are designed to encourage businesses to locate or expand in the enterprise zone, which can help stimulate economic growth and create jobs in the area.

For real estate investors, enterprise zones can be an attractive option due to the potential tax benefits and other incentives that are offered. These benefits can include things like property tax abatements, sales tax exemptions, and income tax credits, among others. These incentives can help reduce the overall cost of investing in real estate in the enterprise zone, which can make it more financially attractive for investors.

In addition to the financial benefits, enterprise zones can offer investors the opportunity to be a part of a community that is actively working to revitalize and improve the area. This can be particularly appealing for investors who are looking to make a positive impact on their community and help drive economic development.

NNN LEASES

A triple net lease, or NNN lease, is a type of commercial real estate lease in which the tenant is responsible for paying all of the operating expenses associated with the property in addition to the rent. These operating expenses can include things like property taxes, insurance, and maintenance and repair costs.

For real estate investors, NNN leases can be an attractive option because they offer a hands-off approach to property management. Under an NNN lease, the investor is essentially just collecting rent, as the tenant is responsible for all of the operating expenses. This can be particularly appealing for investors who do not want to deal with the day-to-day management of a property.

NNN leases can also offer investors a stable, long-term income stream, as the tenant is typically responsible for the property for a set period of time. This can provide a level of predictability and security for the investor.

However, NNN leases can also come with some risks. For example, if the tenant fails to pay the operating expenses, the investor may be required to cover those costs. Additionally, if the property experiences significant maintenance or repair needs, the investor may be required to cover those costs. As a result, it is important for investors to carefully evaluate the tenant's financial stability and the condition of the property before entering into an NNN lease.

CONCLUSION

THE JOURNEY TO BECOMING A REAL ESTATE REALIST

"Success is not final, failure is not fatal: it is the courage to continue that counts."
—Winston Churchill

Congratulations, you have made it to the end of this book and are now equipped with the knowledge, skills, and mindset needed to become a successful real estate investor. Throughout this journey, you have learned the fundamentals of real estate investing, including property analysis, financing, and deal structuring.

In addition, you have gained an understanding of property management, which is essential for maximizing the return on your investments. You now know how to effectively manage properties, build a reliable team, and create systems that streamline the management process.

But beyond the technical aspects of real estate investing, you have also learned how to cultivate a strong mindset and resilience. You now have the tools to overcome fear and self-doubt, embrace change and uncertainty, and deal with setbacks and failures in a constructive way. You have also developed confidence and assertiveness, patience and perseverance, and stress management and self-care strategies to maintain your well-being in this high-stress industry.

Through your continued growth and professional development, you will stay ahead of the curve and succeed in a constantly evolving industry. You will continue to cultivate a growth mindset, embrace challenges as opportunities for growth, and continuously learn and develop new skills and knowledge.

Most importantly, you now have the courage and confidence to take action towards your goals. You are now a real estate realist, ready to take on the world and make yourself a better tomorrow through this mode of investing.

Remember, success is not just about what you know but also about what you do. With the knowledge, skills, and mindset you have gained through this journey, you are now ready to take action towards your dreams and create the life you deserve.

Thank you for joining us on this journey, and we wish you all the best in your real estate investing endeavors. Good luck, and happy investing!

APPENDIX 1

TECH-SAVVY LANDLORDS: LEVERAGING AI, MACHINE LEARNING, AND SOFTWARE

"Technology is anything that wasn't around when
you were born."
—Alan Kay

The current landscape of property management is replete with opportunities for leveraging cutting-edge technology. Artificial intelligence (AI), machine learning, and advanced software applications can streamline various buying, selling, and loan management processes. These innovations can expedite tasks previously consuming hours or days—like determining debt levels, estimating property values, or finding contact information. They can also streamline the coordination and communication among key stakeholders such as tenants, managers, and owners. With each step of the process becoming more efficient, more promising properties can be identified and managed effectively.

As a rental property manager, your income-producing asset is beholden to whoever is on the front lines interacting with your tenants, such as your property management company. The best way to ensure that your property satisfies your residents' needs is to find an employee who never sleeps and knows all the answers before they are asked. This is where the advent of AI software can help. The success of a rental property manager hinges largely on those engaging with the tenants—like the property management company. An ideal scenario is having a resource that never sleeps and can answer queries before they're even asked. Enter AI.

Artificial intelligence, machine learning, and other modern software can also help throughout the process of buying and selling real estate and dealing with loans. It can help investors research in minutes that would have previously taken hours or days, such as figuring out debt levels, property values, and contact information. It helps you organize and communicate with important parties, like tenants, managers, and owners. The more time you save at every step of the process, the more properties you will be able to find and comfortably keep in your portfolio.

TENANT MANAGEMENT

Most of the questions your chatbot receives will be simple, recurring ones that almost everyone asks. "Are pets allowed in the apartment? How much is the rent for a two-bedroom unit? Are washer and dryer included?" There is only a relatively small amount that requires some real thought. The bot only needs to recognize a few keywords in sequence to know what kind of answer to give. The more exposure AI has to these types of inquiries, the better it gets at coming up with satisfactory answers to them. Similar programs can handle recurring communication tasks like emailing tenants, reminding them that their payment is due, processing requests, and so on.

As AI continues to penetrate our society at an explosive rate following the popularity of OpenAI's ChatGPT, the use cases for these chatbots continue to grow more sophisticated and useful for business purposes. At the time of writing in 2023, we're now experimenting with ChatGPT-based chatbots for our property management business that are able to respond in real-time to customer queries with unique and thoughtful answers to their questions that go beyond routine questions we manually programmed into a database. This is allowing us to provide a greater level of service to our existing tenants and streamline the process of acquiring new tenants. Our staff have to spend less time answering questions from prospective tenants, and their calendars are filling up with appointments to show properties the AI bots set for them.

Various rental property software platforms enable tenants to do routine activities more conveniently, such as paying their rent and making maintenance requests online. By taking the time to learn and implement the right management software, you may even be able to cut out a large portion of the regular property management duties and give greater transparency about how your building is being operated.

Landlords can use property management software, such as TenantCloud, to provide tenants with an online portal where they can access information about their unit and the property, pay rent, request maintenance, and communicate with the landlord or property manager. These portals can help tenants feel more connected and empowered, as they have a central place to access the information and services they need.

COST MANAGEMENT

Usually, if you go to a hotel, you'll only be able to adjust the thermostat up or down to a certain temperature. That's because the management doesn't want guests driving up the electrical bill. The right software will enable you to implement a similar system in all your units, which could save you a lot on recurring utility charges if you're the one covering them. Some people will just refuse to put on a sweater so long as they can adjust the heat to any absurd number they want and not have to deal with the bill themselves.

Smart home technologies also allow you and/or your tenants to remotely monitor many important aspects of a unit. With the right program, you can know when doors are accessed from a smartphone so that you will know who goes in and out. You can assign codes that change with each use to each door. This is useful, for instance, if a maintenance worker needs to access a unit and the tenant is not available to be there at that particular time. They can just give the worker a one-time use code to let themselves in.

With smart air conditioners, heating, and ventilation systems, tenants can have their units automatically adjust to their preferred settings when they are home and shut off when they are not. This will make them more comfortable at home and save on utility costs for everyone. In a similar way, lights throughout units and common areas can be preprogrammed to optimal settings and automatically turned off when unoccupied.

Smart technology and the internet of things open up new options for routine upkeep and maintenance. With the right sensors calibrated in the right places around your property, you'll be able to thoroughly monitor and predict what needs to be replaced or fixed next. Deterioration through everyday use is easy to keep track of, and it makes it less likely that something crucial will fail and start causing you lost revenue and unhappy tenants.

ENERGY EFFICIENCY AND SUSTAINABILITY

Another area where technology can be useful in rental property management is in the area of energy efficiency and sustainability. With the increasing focus on environmental sustainability and the rising cost of energy, landlords have a strong incentive to make their rental properties as energy-efficient as possible.

There are a number of technology tools and resources that landlords can use to improve the energy efficiency of their rental properties. This is another area where smart home devices can help landlords reduce energy consumption. Smart thermostats, smart lights, and smart appliances are all in a smart landlord's arsenal of management tools. These technologies can allow tenants to control and monitor energy use in their units and can help reduce overall energy costs for the property.

In addition to smart home technologies, landlords can also use property management software, such as Building Engines, to track and manage energy consumption across their properties. These systems can provide landlords with real-time energy usage data and help them identify improvement opportunities and cost savings.

SAFETY AND SECURITY

One area where technology can be particularly useful in rental property management is in the area of security and safety. Ensuring the safety and security of rental properties is essential for landlords, as it helps protect the value of their investments and ensure the well-being of their tenants.

There are a number of technology tools and resources that landlords can use to improve the security of their rental properties. For example, landlords can use smart home technologies, such as smart locks, security cameras, and smoke detectors, to monitor and secure their properties. These technologies can alert landlords to potential issues, such as break-ins or fires, and provide them with real-time visibility into what is happening on their properties.

MARKETING AND LEASING

One area where technology can be particularly useful in rental property management is in the area of marketing and leasing. With the proliferation of online platforms and tools, it is now easier than ever for landlords to reach potential tenants and showcase their properties.

For example, landlords can use online listing sites like Zillow, Trulia, and HotPads to advertise their rental properties to a wide audience. These platforms allow landlords to include detailed descriptions, photos, and videos of their properties and information about location, amenities, and rental terms.

Another way that technology can be used in rental property management is through the use of virtual tours. With the use of 360-degree cameras and virtual reality technology, landlords can now offer potential tenants the ability to explore their properties remotely without the need for in-person showings. This can be a particularly useful tool in the current environment, where social distancing measures may make in-person showings more difficult.

MAINTENANCE AND REPAIRS

Another important aspect of rental property management is maintenance and repairs. Properly maintaining a rental property is essential for ensuring the safety, comfort, and satisfaction of tenants and preserving the property's value. As previously discussed, this process can be made easier by using AI chatbots in conjunction with software like Buildium to manage repair requests.

One of the biggest challenges of rental property management is ensuring that properties are occupied with reliable tenants. Vacant units can be costly, as they generate no income and may require additional expenses for marketing and repairs.

To help reduce vacancy rates and improve tenant retention, landlords can use technology to screen potential tenants and manage the leasing process. For example, landlords can use online platforms like Cozy to advertise their rental properties, collect applications, and conduct background and credit checks on potential tenants. These platforms can also help landlords automate leasing, including generating leases, tracking rent payments, and managing move-ins and move-outs.

Landlords can also use social media and online reviews to learn more about potential tenants and get a sense of their reputation and reliability. By leveraging these tools and technologies, landlords can make more informed decisions about which tenants to approve and improve their chances of filling their units with reliable renters.

You can have the most common and useful inputs built into chat robots on your website. A tenant can log on to your system and type, "I have a plumbing leak. Who do I call?" The chat robot will recognize combinations of certain key terms in their inquiry as well as predetermined information about the tenant. "Hi. Thanks for that question, Nathan. I see that you are at 1162 #18. This is the phone number for our primary plumber. You can go to our second or third option if he's unavailable. For the quickest response, please post your photo with your phone into our software app, Buildium. We can send that to one of our three plumbers and get someone out to your unit to fix it. Otherwise, they can call you and explain to you how to solve the problem yourself."

REGULATIONS

In addition to the operational and management tasks involved in rental property investing, landlords also need to be aware of the legal and regulatory requirements that apply to their properties. These requirements can vary widely depending on the location of the property, the type of rental, and other factors.

To help landlords stay compliant with these requirements, several tools and resources are available. For example, landlords can use online platforms like Avail to access and review state and local rental laws and regulations. These platforms can also guide landlords on how to comply with these requirements, such as by providing forms and templates for leases and other legal documents.

Landlords can also use software, such as Buildium, to manage their rental properties' financial and accounting aspects. These systems can help landlords track income and expenses, generate reports and tax documents, and manage rent payments and other financial transactions.

RECORD KEEPING

One of the key challenges of rental property management is maintaining accurate and up-to-date records. Landlords need to keep track of a wide range of information, including financial transactions, legal documents, maintenance and repair records, and tenant information.

Traditionally, this has required a lot of manual effort, including tracking and organizing paper documents, manually inputting data into spreadsheets, and manually reconciling financial records. However, with the advent of technology, many of these tasks can now be automated and streamlined.

For example, landlords can use property management software, such as AppFolio, to centralize and manage all of their rental property records in one place. These systems can provide landlords with a secure and organized way to store and access all of their important documents, including leases, contracts, invoices, and financial records.

NAVIGATING THE REGULATORY LANDSCAPE: TENANT ISSUES TO ENVIRONMENTAL CONCERNS AND ECONOMIC UNCERTAINTY

"In any moment of decision, the best thing you can do is the right thing, the next best thing is the wrong thing, and the worst thing you can do is nothing."
—Theodore Roosevelt.

One potential challenge that rental property owners may encounter is the involvement of attorneys and free legal aid sources that claim to protect tenants. While their intentions may seem noble, these interactions can lead to adversarial situations that drain the hard-earned assets of new property owners.

Various legal protections exist to assist residents in retaining their rental units without incurring additional costs.

With older buildings, it's essential to consider the historical elements that may be present. These properties may have been constructed when materials with health risks were commonly used. Asbestos, once widely utilized as a fire retardant, can be found in vinyl sheet flooring. Lead-based paint may also be present, adding a touch of historic authenticity to the walls. Formaldehyde can be found in certain types of wood, while polybutylene pipes and electromagnetic radiation from power lines were once commonplace. Water leaks can lead to the growth of mold, which requires careful attention. While it's crucial to understand the risks associated with these substances, it's equally important to approach the topic with a balanced perspective and seek accurate information.

If you own an older building, someone may be looking to use any of the above possibilities to seek a payout. Just the accusation itself can cause all kinds of public relations nightmares for you and your building. If somebody falls at your property and claims that they tripped on an improperly placed sprinkler, suddenly, it's your burden to figure out how to fix it and to avoid getting sued. That's why I hold my properties in limited liability companies (LLCs). If I do get sued, the amount they come after me for is only the amount in that property and nothing else. The LLC remits the liability to that property. I've even taken it a step further and chosen a different state (Wyoming) to base my LLCs.

An LLC is a type of legal structure that can be used to protect the personal assets of its owners or members from the liabilities of the business. LLCs can be set up as single-member or multiple-member entities, depending on the number of owners involved. In Wyoming, the only remedy if somebody wins in court against my LLC is to get a charging order, which means they can get a partial ownership interest in my property. Normally, that would sound like a bad thing. The reason it's a good thing is that I'm still the manager of the property or the LLC. I can make that property lose money or incur a phantom tax liability, meaning that the owner that wins a lawsuit against me gets to own part of the property. I can then stab myself in the gut, and they get stabbed with me.

Wyoming LLC law does not allow any room for legal interpretation:

"On application by a judgment creditor of a member or transferee, a court may enter a charging order against the transferable interest of the judgment debtor for the unsatisfied amount of the judgment. A charging order requires the limited liability company to pay over to the person to whom the charging order was issued any distribution that would otherwise be paid to the judgment debtor."

What's nice about this wording is that it means a person seeking to enforce a legal judgment against you as the property owner can only hold an ownership interest in this particular limited liability company, not your personal wealth. They cannot manage or direct in any way how that limited liability company is run.

Attorneys typically don't want their clients to end up losing money, and that's what these protections help promote. I can turn around and sell the property for a loss. I can make it so that the other party owes the IRS taxes. When they don't actually have income, it's called phantom tax liability. That is a fun way to lay a landmine for unscrupulous actors who try to mess with me. Phantom tax liability refers to the potential tax consequences of certain types of transactions or events that do not involve the transfer of cash. This can occur when the value of a non-cash asset, such as stock or real estate, increases and the owner realizes a gain on the sale of the asset. In this case, the owner may owe taxes on the gain even though no cash has changed hands.

For example, if an individual owns a piece of rental property that appreciates in value over time, they may owe taxes on the appreciation when they sell the property, even if they use the proceeds from the sale to purchase a new property. Similarly, if an individual receives stock as part of their compensation from an employer and the stock increases in value, they may owe taxes on the appreciation when they sell the stock, even if they do not receive any cash from the sale.

To make things worse, the local city guidance can be limited in explaining how to resolve problems. Many city personnel are overworked and underpaid. On one occasion, I was ordered to put in a new heater, but the type of heater wasn't specified, and no one I spoke to about the issue was able to elaborate. I incurred significant unnecessary fees trying to get clarity on the issue and avoid greater city pressure for failing to comply. On another occasion, an aid for the city walked my property after a neighbor complained about the condition. They wanted me to bring my building up to their stan-dards, even though every other property on the block was the same. Thanks to this bureaucratic overstep, I ended up having to put a lot of money into the property for reasons I did not fully understand nor see a clear return on.

Possibly the most harmful and egregious example of bureaucratic over-reaching into rental property owners' lives comes in the form of an eviction moratorium. If you own a restaurant, and you're forced for reasons beyond your control to temporarily lose that restaurant, it frees you up for the time being from the costs and responsibilities of running it. You stop making gains, but you've also mostly halted your losses. You're not getting paid anymore, but your time and capital are at least freed up to focus on other financial pur-suits. If, however, as a restaurateur, you are forced to continue to feed people without getting paid for your food, you're quickly going to run that restaurant into the ground. It's simply not sustainable nor in your interest as the owner. Eviction moratoriums are like that situation for rental property owners.

There can be times (like during the COVID-19 pandemic) when bureau-crats and lawmakers will require you to house your tenants and manage your property, even if they don't pay their rent. You can't evict them, no matter what problems they cause or how much they drain your finances. The larg-er, experienced property owners can handle this burden for a while. But the financial burden placed upon individual mom-and-pop and first-time proper-ty owners can be life-ruining. Banks don't like having people not pay their loans.

With a rental property loan, it is generally expected that the money used to pay off the loan comes from rental income. The loan agreement usually requires it. If you have to use other sources of income to make loan payments, it may violate the terms of your agreement, which could affect your ability to borrow money in the future. This poses an obvious problem if you have no rental income for an extended period. Carefully review your agreement's terms and conditions. If you have any questions or concerns, seek advice from a real estate attorney or financial advisor.

It's a very unfair and messed up situation for rental property owners. They still have all of their expenses but no income to cover those expenses. The tax authorities require them to pay their property taxes, too. So, they can either cough up the money if they have enough savings or be forced into financial mishaps by providing others a place to live during difficult times. It's horrible.

And even when your tenants are still paying you each month, you might be legally prevented from charging as much as the market equilibrium allows for or the minimum you need to keep operating at a profit. In many cities around the US, there are a lot of rent control laws keeping rental prices artificially low. As a result, not many people are investing in rental properties and making more living spaces available to people. As the population grows in these places, there's going to be greater demand for the relatively small amount of units. Every unit will fill up as soon as it becomes available, and there won't be enough units to go around.

APPENDIX 3

INNOVATIVE INVESTMENT STRATEGIES: THE FUTURE OF RENTALS

"The only constant in life is change."
—Heraclitus

In the ever-changing landscape of the rental property industry, it's important to stay informed about emerging trends and opportunities.

CO-LIVING AND CO-HOUSING

Co-living and co-housing are innovative and popular ways of living that have gained traction in recent years. These models offer a unique and community-oriented living experience, with shared spaces and amenities that help create a sense of community and belonging.

With co-living, each tenant will have their own private bedroom, but they will share communal spaces such as kitchens, living rooms, and bathrooms. This model is popular among millennials and young professionals looking for a more affordable and communal living experience.

Co-housing, on the other hand, involves a group living in a community designed to foster social interaction and cooperation. These communities typically have shared common spaces, such as gardens, playgrounds, and community centers. Residents share in the responsibilities of managing and maintaining the community, which can include tasks like cooking, cleaning, and maintenance work.

As a rental real estate investor, investing in co-living and co-housing properties can be a smart move. These properties offer a range of benefits, including higher rental yields, lower vacancy rates, and lower turnover rates. Additionally, the shared amenities and community-oriented living experience can be very attractive to tenants, particularly millennials and young professionals.

My brother Josh also took the co-housing concept and built a 4-unit house from scratch in a favela in Rio de Janeiro. His house offers a unique experience, views that inspire envy, an in-home gym, a yoga studio, and a greenhouse. He fosters a community of adventurous digital nomads who seek a deeper experience than what they would find by renting in more touristy neighborhoods on Airbnb.

In terms of sustainable and eco-friendly design, the Treehouse co-living community in Brooklyn, New York, is a great example. This community features 21 apartments, each with its own private bathroom and shared common spaces. The building is designed to be energy-efficient, with features like solar panels, rainwater harvesting, and a green roof. The community also hosts regular workshops and events focused on sustainability and eco-friendly living.

Furthermore, co-living and co-housing properties offer rental real estate investors the opportunity to diversify their investment portfolios. These properties can provide a steady stream of rental income, which can be particularly attractive in areas with high demand for affordable housing.

In addition, co-living and co-housing communities can be designed and managed sustainably and eco-friendly, which can be a major selling point for environmentally conscious tenants. By incorporating features such as energy-efficient design, green roofs, and solar panels, rental real estate investors can appeal to tenants who are looking for more sustainable and eco-friendly living options.

Moreover, the COVID-19 pandemic has highlighted the benefits of co-living and co-housing communities, as tenants can feel more socially connected and supported during times of isolation and uncertainty. This has led to a surge in demand for co-living and co-housing properties, making them a potentially lucrative investment opportunity for rental real estate investors.

SHORT-TERM AND VACATION RENTALS

The short-term and vacation rental market has become a major trend in the real estate industry, providing rental real estate investors with a unique opportunity to generate higher rental yields by renting out their properties for short stays. The growth of platforms like Airbnb and Vrbo has made it easier than ever for investors to list their properties and reach a wider audience.

One of the key benefits of short-term rentals is the ability to charge higher nightly rates than traditional long-term rentals. This can be particularly lucrative in popular tourist destinations, where demand for short-term rentals is high. Additionally, short-term rentals can help to reduce vacancy rates and generate more income for investors during the off-season.

However, it's important for rental real estate investors to research and comply with local regulations and laws regarding short-term rentals. Many cities and states have specific regulations and zoning laws in place to govern short-term rentals, and failure to comply with these laws can result in hefty fines and legal issues.

Despite the potential legal hurdles, short-term and vacation rentals remain a lucrative opportunity for rental real estate investors. By carefully researching and complying with local regulations, investors can generate higher rental yields and attract a wider range of tenants. Some successful examples of short-term rentals include The Guild, Sonder, and Lyric, all of which offer stylish, fully-furnished apartments in popular tourist destinations.

IMPACT AND SOCIALLY RESPONSIBLE INVESTING

Impact and socially responsible investing are becoming increasingly popular among investors seeking to positively impact society and the environment. There are many opportunities to invest in properties that align with ethical, social, and environmental standards.

Impact investing can take many forms, such as investing in properties built using sustainable materials or properties that provide affordable housing for low-income individuals and families. Impact investing can also involve investing in properties that positively impact the environment, such as using renewable energy sources or promoting sustainable living.

Socially responsible investing also offers many opportunities for rental real estate investors. This type of investing involves investing in companies or properties that align with ethical, social, and environmental standards. This could include investing in affordable housing properties or promoting sustainable living.

By investing in impact and socially responsible properties, rental real estate investors can generate financial returns and contribute to a better world. These investments can help address pressing social and environmental issues and offer attractive financial returns.

AFFORDABLE HOUSING AND GOVERNMENT PROGRAMS

Affordable housing has become an increasingly pressing issue in many cities and countries worldwide. With rising housing costs and stagnant wages, many individuals and families struggle to find affordable and stable housing. As a result, governments have introduced various programs and incentives to encourage the development of affordable housing projects.

As a rental real estate investor, investing in affordable housing projects can be smart. These properties are often in high demand and can offer steady rental income streams. Additionally, tax benefits and other incentives are often available to investors who participate in these programs.

One example of a successful government-backed affordable housing program is the Low-Income Housing Tax Credit (LIHTC) in the United States. This program provides tax credits to developers who build or renovate affordable housing properties. The credits can then be sold to investors, providing an additional source of financing for the project. The LIHTC program has been instrumental in the development of affordable housing projects across the country.

ADAPTIVE REUSE

Adaptive reuse is a term used to describe the process of repurposing existing buildings or structures for a different use than what they were originally designed for. It allows for the preservation and revitalization of historically and architecturally significant buildings. By repurposing these structures, their unique character and charm can be maintained, contributing to the cultural fabric of a community.

In many cases, adaptive reuse can be a cost-effective alternative to new construction because existing buildings often have infrastructure and foundational elements in place to reduce construction and development costs compared to building from scratch. This approach also minimizes waste, reduces energy consumption, preserves valuable resources, and saves time compared to the lengthy process of designing and constructing a new building.

Adaptive reuse can help create more diverse and affordable housing options in various locations and building types or revitalize underutilized or neglected areas, bringing new economic and social opportunities to these areas. They can often be completed more quickly than new construction, as it does not require the same lengthy planning and approvals process. Adaptive reuse projects often result in unique, character-filled rental spaces that stand out in the market. These distinctive spaces can attract tenants looking for something different and create a competitive advantage for property owners.

Adaptive reuse projects can help increase property values in the surrounding area, which can benefit both property owners and the community. They also create short-term jobs during the construction and rehabilitation process and permanent jobs once the project is completed.

APPENDIX 4

NETWORKING, PROFESSIONAL DEVELOPMENT, AND THE FUTURE OF REAL ESTATE INVESTING

"Your brand is what other people say about you when you're not in the room."
—Jeff Bezos

Real estate investing is a relationship-based business, and building and maintaining strong connections is essential for long-term success. Networking and building a power team are critical components of this business, and they can help investors identify new investment opportunities, gain access to financing, and build their reputation in the industry.

NETWORKING AND BUILDING
A POWER TEAM

One of the primary benefits of networking is the opportunity to gain access to new investment opportunities and potential partners. Real estate agents, for example, can provide information about off-market properties and assist in the buying and selling process. Attorneys can provide legal advice and assist with contracts, while lenders can offer financing options for investment properties.

Long before you feel that you're ready to make your first investment, you can begin to assemble your power team. Meeting with people who work in the business and its related components daily will give you a fuller picture of what goes into real estate investing. You will also build up your confidence by hearing stories from experienced professionals and knowing who you can call when you have issues and need advice. A power team might include a real estate agent, attorney, lender, property manager, contractor, accountant, and insurance agent. Each member of the team can provide specialized knowledge and expertise, and collectively, they can help investors identify and manage risks associated with real estate investments.

Networking can also help investors develop relationships with other professionals who can provide valuable insight and advice. Property managers, for example, can assist with tenant screening, rent collection, and property maintenance, while contractors can provide estimates for repairs and renovations. By surrounding themselves with a team of trusted professionals, investors can leverage their expertise to help mitigate risks and maximize returns.

ADAPTING TO CHANGES IN
REAL ESTATE INVESTMENT

The real estate industry is always evolving, and investors who cannot keep up with the changes risk being left behind. Changes in technology, government regulations, and the economy can all significantly impact the real estate market, and investors need to be prepared to adapt to these changes.

One recent example in America is the implementation of Opportunity Zones. This new legislation that came into effect under the Trump administration provides real estate investors certain tax incentives for buying real estate in certain areas and fulfilling certain conditions. Allowing investors to erase some of their capital gains exposure

Technological advances have also led to the rise of online real estate platforms, making it easier for investors to find and invest in properties. Investors unfamiliar with these platforms may miss out on opportunities that their competitors are taking advantage of. Similarly, changes in government regulations can affect the tax implications of real estate investments and the legal requirements for owning and managing properties.

Moreover, economic changes can majorly impact the real estate market. For instance, during times of economic downturn, property values may decline, and demand for rental properties may decrease. Investors who are not prepared to adapt to these changes may find themselves struggling to stay afloat in the industry.

Therefore, real estate investors must stay informed about changes in the market and be prepared to adapt their strategies accordingly. They can do this by attending industry conferences, keeping up-to-date with industry news and publications, and networking with other professionals in the industry. They can seek ongoing education and training in various business areas to ensure they have the skills and knowledge needed to succeed in the ever-changing real estate market.

BRANDING AND MARKETING FOR REAL ESTATE INVESTORS

Branding and marketing are crucial components of success for real estate investors. In order to stand out in a competitive industry, investors must develop a strong brand identity and marketing strategy. This begins with creating a professional website that showcases their properties and services.

In addition to a website, real estate investors can utilize social media platforms such as Facebook, Twitter, and Instagram to connect with potential clients and partners. These platforms allow investors to engage with their audience and build relationships with potential clients. Real estate investors can also utilize email marketing to stay in touch with their audience and promote their properties and services. This involves building an email list of potential clients and sending out regular newsletters and updates.

The most important brand, however, is your reputation. When you decide to enter into the endeavor of real estate investing, it is important that you act mindfully on how your reputation is going to be perceived by lenders, agents, and brokers. If you waste people's time by walking into deals without having done your research, or don't have everything in order when the time comes to actually make an offer, you may earn the reputation of an amateur or someone who is unserious.

Made in the USA
Middletown, DE
10 September 2024

60055501R00109